G000270957

BIRMINGHAM:
MORE OF THE
SIXTIES

Alton & Jo Douglas

Best Wishes
Alton & Jo

Rush hour snarl-up at Five Ways junction, looking along Hagley Road, 13th October 1966.

© 2010 Alton and Jo Douglas
ISBN 978-1-85858-467-6
Published by Brewin Books Ltd., Doric House, 56 Alcester Road, Studley, Warwickshire B80 7LG.
Printed by Warwick Printing Co. Ltd., Caswell Road, Leamington Spa CV31 1QD.
Layout by Alton and Jo Douglas
All Rights Reserved

The end is nigh for Paddington Street, Hockley, 11th April 1960.

Front Cover: The modernisation of New Street Station is underway, 19th October 1964.

Contents

BREWIN BOOKS LTD

Doric House, 56 Alcester Road,
Studley, Warwickshire B80 7LG

Tel: 01527 854228 Fax: 01527 852746

Vat Registration No. 705 0077 73

Dear Nostalgic,

Look, I don't want to begin by arguing with you, but I won't agree with your choice and that's that! You see, when we look at our books we all start selecting our personal favourites, so I thought I'd start by highlighting a few of mine.

First of all there's that superb aerial shot of New Street Station on the cover – not bad, eh? There's an all-action photo of the Town Hall; Albert Street bringing back memories of the walk down to The Beehive and that picture of the much-loved fountain in Chamberlain Square. But, what about Colonnade Passage – how many of you can remember that? Then there are the preparations for Camp Hill flyover and its completion; the rear of Heneage Street (what images of other back street courtyards that conjures up!) and the visits to the city by Frank Sinatra Jnr., the Everly Brothers and Ella Fitzgerald all recalled. Oh and before I forget, my favourite advertisement is one of the smallest in the book - it's on Page 94 for entertainer, Madge E Kwand (I wonder what her real name was? Or perhaps, that's it!).

Anyway, enough of my favourite "recalls" - how about yours? I bet we end up disagreeing, but with more than 350 items to choose from, who cares? Whoever thought falling out could be such fun!

Yours, in friendship,

Alton

Representatives from 15 overseas countries attend a reception given by the Lord Mayor, Ald G Corbyn Barrow, to mark
Meet the People Week, Council House, 3rd November 1965.

1960

SLEEP-LEARNING

Learn while you sleep
for 11 plus, GCE, Professional
Qualifications, Languages, etc.

APPLY FOR DETAILS OF MEMBERSHIP,
EQUIPMENT, TAPES,

THE SOCIETY FOR HYPNOPAEDIA

'Londesborough House', 79 Hollie Lucas Road,

Kings Heath, Birmingham, 13. Highbury 4029

For all Sports, touring or racing Motor cycles...

.... go to

COUNTY

CYCLE & MOTOR CO. LTD.
266. BROAD ST., BIRMINGHAM 1. MID 2671
266. STRATFORD RD., SHIRLEY. SHI 1530
(Opposite Shirley Odeon)

BSA 250 STAR SCRAMBLER
JOINT BIRMINGHAM DISTRIBUTORS
FOR B.S.A.

1960 SHOWROOM SCRAMBLE

1.ST - PETER TAFT

NO NEED TO SCRAMBLE ROUND THE SHOWROOMS TRYING TO FIND A GOOD MACHINE.—IN 1st PLACE IS PETER TAFT, WHERE YOU WILL BE SURE OF FINDING NOTHING BUT THE BEST IN ROAD AND COMPETITION MOTOR CYCLES AND SCOOTERS

SPARES and REPAIRS

Peter Taft

TERMS and EXCHANGES

1308-10 Pershore Road,
Stirchley, Birmingham 30

On 27, 41 and 45 Bus Routes from Town.   Phone: KIN 3384

Coventry Road/Charles Road, Small Heath, 8th February 1960.

1. The Frantic
   FREDDY LLOYD FIVE

2. Your Compere
   TONY MARSH

3. H.M.V.'s New Rock Pesonality
   DANNY HUNTER *supported by*
   The Fabulous FLEE-RAKKERS

4. Pye's New Disc Star
   LANCE ($^{BE}_{MINE}$) FORTUNE

5. TONY MARSH *introduces*

6. The Fabulous
   FIVE DALLAS BOYS

   Interval

7. Triumph Records All-Star Rock Group
   The Fabulous FLEE-RAKKERS *with* JIMMY BARRON

8. Organ Star from "Oh Boy" & "Boy Meets Girls"
   CHERRY WAINER *with* DON STORER

9. TONY MARSH

10. America's most consistent Stars of the Hit Parade
    THE EVERLY BROTHERS

God save the Queen

The Everly Brothers, Odeon, New Street, March 1960.

American rock 'n roll star, Eddie Cochran, Hippodrome, March 1960. The following month he was killed in a car crash.

The Birmingham **Mail**

comes home to you

WITH ALL THE DAY'S NEWS

ATLAS BALLROOM BINGO
FLAXLEY ROAD, STECHFORD
THE ATLAS
Now offers you £7,500 in Prize Money

Lucky *Scoop*

Over £1,200 to be won nightly.
Over £6,000 to be won weekly.
USUAL THREE LARGE SNOWBALLS
Doors open 7 p.m.   Bingo commences 7.45 p.m.

Union Street, looking towards High Street, 1960.

any message
any distance
any time

TEL - STOR

TELEPHONE
ANSWERING
& RECORDING
MACHINE

receives your calls
24 hours a day.
Records any
conversation on your
Telephone and serves
you as a
Dictating Machine

●

SHIPTON AUTOMATION (SALES) LIMITED.
NORFOLK HOUSE, SMALLBROOK,
RINGWAY, BIRMINGHAM, 5.
TEL: MIDLAND 4 6 6 1
A MEMBER OF THE SHIPTON GROUP OF COMPANIES

Dale End, 25th March 1960.

Henry Street/Lupin Street, Bloomsbury, April 1960.

Hunters Road, Hockley, 26th May 1960.

Chick's Café, Tyburn Road, Erdington, 1960.

JOHN O. HOLT & SON LTD
STEEL SHEETS · TINPLATES · BLACKPLATES
RECOGNISED STOCKHOLDERS FOR
JOHN SUMMERS & SONS LTD

22 GEORGE ROAD
BIRMINGHAM 15
Phone : EDG 5226/9

New Street, Erdington, 11th August 1960.

Gravelly Lane, Erdington, 1960.

THE BIRMINGHAM
REPERTORY THEATRE

In association with
THE ARTS COUNCIL OF GREAT BRITAIN

presents

on Tuesday, September 27th

for a season

ONE WAY PENDULUM

by N. F. SIMPSON

An evening of high drung and slarrit

CHARACTERS

in order of appearance

KIRBY GROOMKIRBY	IAN FROST
ROBERT BARNES	.. JOHN CARLIN
MABEL GROOMKIRBY ..	ELIZABETH SPRIGGS
SYLVIA GROOMKIRBY ..	.. ROSEMARY LEACH
AUNT MILDRED	.. BRENDA JONES
MYRA GANTRY	HILARY LIDDELL
ARTHUR GROOMKIRBY	ARTHUR PENTELOW
STANLEY HONEYBLOCK ..	DEREK JACOBI
JUDGE	.. PETER WYATT
PROSECUTING COUNSEL ..	BERNARD KILBY
DEFENDING COUNSEL ..	.. JOHN ROLFE
USHER	RONALD FALK
CLERK OF THE COURT.. ..	JOHN FORGHAM
POLICEMAN	BRIAN BLESSED

The Play directed by BERNARD HEPTON

The Setting designed by DIANA DEWES

A limited number of symbolic overtones is available free to those requiring
them for personal consumption only. They are NOT for re-sale to the public

Ian Menzies and the Clyde Valley Stompers take off at the All-night Jazz Festival, Town Hall, September 1960.

The White Hart, Railway Terrace/Nechells Park Road, 17th October 1960.

Scholefield Street/Great Lister Street, Nechells, 18th October 1960.

Broadstone Road, Yardley, 4th November 1960.

CANDY & MORRIS
LIMITED

Builders' Merchants

———

SHIRLEY, BIRMINGHAM

———

Telephone: SHirley 1114 (3 lines)

ALLEN ROWLAND
& CO. LTD.

SCRAP
IRON, STEEL and
NON-FERROUS METALS

● *All Grades Purchased*
● *Birmingham's Largest Buyers*

680 WARWICK ROAD, TYSELEY, BIRMINGHAM, 11

Telephones:
ACOcks Green 1110 & 3410   BEArwood 1557 & 1254

WIMBUSH
AND
WORTH-WHILE

———

HIGH-CLASS CONFECTIONERY AND BREADS

WEDDING CAKES AND BIRTHDAY CAKES A SPECIALITY

A. D. WIMBUSH & SON LTD.
SMALL HEATH, BIRMINGHAM

Shops and Agents throughout the Midlands

Radio
Television
and Repairs

Stockists of
G.E.C.

Electrical
Contracting
Members of
E.C.A. and
N.I.C.E.I.C.

WALTER R. SELL
20 WASHWOOD HEATH ROAD, BIRMINGHAM, 8.

PHONE EAST 0862

KEPPEL'S (B'HAM) LTD.,
3 Washwood Heath Road, Birmingham 8   EAS 3395

WE ARE THE SINK UNIT AND FIREPLACE SPECIALISTS
We have a large range of Sink Units from £8 to £60 and Fireplaces from £8 to £45

ANNOUNCING NEW ALL STEEL BATH COMPLETE WITH BATH PANELS AND TAPS. ALL COLOURS ONLY £17 10s.

Bull Street, 16th November 1960.

Carrs Lane, 23rd November 1960.

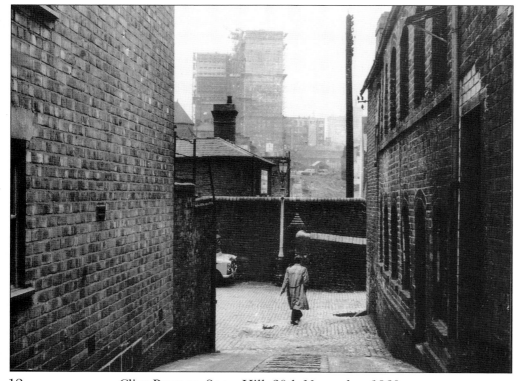

A. H. WOODCOCK

Mortgage & Insurance Broker

Beacon Cinema Buildings,

**Birmingham Road,
Great Barr.
Phone GRE 2272**

Mortgages for purchase of Houses, Flats or Businesses. Quickly arranged with free life insurance (up to 35 years).

Car Insurance 50% N.C.B. after 3 years.

Clive Passage, Snow Hill, 30th November 1960.

Come and discuss your choice of a –
at

Colliers

SOLE DISTRIBUTORS FOR THE GREATER BIRMINGHAM AREA

R. H. COLLIER & CO. LTD., 42 Easy Row, B'ham 1. *Tel. MID 2317*

Bright Street, Aston, December 1960.

Cateswell Road, Hall Green, 3rd December 1960.

Rear of Kilmorie Road, Acocks Green, 12th December 1960.

13

Colonnade Passage, which ran from New Street to Stephenson Street, 6th January 1961.

LATEST FROM CANADA

WEISER LOCKS

A happy trend of Canadian Front Door Furniture moves East. Many in the West are adopting these rather distinctive patterns over here. Why not glamourise your doors? Ask for List WYL 708.

ENTRANCE LOCKS
Backset 2¾" A500 58/8 set
" 2½" A501 58/8 set
KEY IN KNOB for use with all types of Entrance Doors.

1641
Cast Star 9¾" x 7¾"
Escutcheon
(or Backplate) only
61/- each.

1636
6" x 12" Escutcheon
(or Backplate) only
40/10 each.

PWA **PARKER, WINDER & ACHURCH LTD.**
708 BERKLEY ST. CORNER, BROAD ST., BIRMINGHAM 1
ALSO AT LONDON & MANCHESTER

Telephone
MIDland 3001
Telegrams:
"Ironclad" B'ham 1

SYLVANDALE SHOPS
for Service and Selection

Smarts

HAM-BACON
Famous for COOKED MEATS
SAUSAGES

W. H. SMART & CO. LTD., BRISTOL RD., BIRMINGHAM 29

If in doubt
KEMP *will help you out!*
For your next
Motor Cycle, Scooter or Three Wheeler,

see **R. G. KEMP**
at
87 Redhill Road, West Heath, Birmingham 31
PRIory 4100

STOP! at **BROADMEADOW**
for

MOTOR CYCLES
MO-PEDS
SCOOTERS
SIDE CARS

All the latest models and colours
Easy H.P. Terms
Part Exchanges
Spares and Accessories
for all makes

9 & 11 WATFORD ROAD, COTTERIDGE, BIRMINGHAM 30.
Tel.: KIN 3408.
IN ASSOCIATION WITH THE SCOOTER SHOP, AND ELWOODS.

METAL DUCTS LTD

Tel. VICTORIA 5881-2

DOMINION WORKS, ALFRED RD.
SPARKHILL, BIRMINGHAM·11

VENTILATION, DUST EXTRACTION
FUME REMOVAL, DUCTING,
TANKS, FABRICATED STEELWORK

Demolition work at Six Ways, with Alma Street on the left, Aston, 27th February 1961.

15

Wheway Optical Co.Ltd., Barr Street, Newtown, February 1961.

Kingsbury Road, Erdington, 1961.

ANODISING
|means|
HAYNES, FORD
& ELLIOTT LTD.

ANODISING
PRESSWORK
SPRAY PAINTING
POLISHING
& WELDING

PRITCHETT ST. ASTON
BIRMINGHAM · 6
PHONE · ASTON CROSS 3511

Lombard Finishing Co. Ltd. 20/24
Lombard st 12

Lustre Finish Anodising Co.

LUSTRE PHONE
CENTRAL
8170
FINISH ANODISING CO.
POLISHING - PLATING - ANODISING
BARREL POLISHING TO THE TRADE
LANCASTER WKS., CAMDEN DR., BIRMINGHAM, I.

Personal Attention **BIRMINGHAM SCHOOL OF** Patience & Courtesy
STANDARD & ADVANCED DRIVING

Due to a high percentage of Passes, this School is again able to accept a limited number of pupils for enrolment on the Standard Driving Course.

Also available are Courses:—
(a) To M.O.T. Test standard for Provisional Licence holders with some experience.
(b) To I.A.M. Test standard for Full Licence holders with not less than 3 years' regular driving experience (Object — to increase present margin of safety).

GUARANTEE
You will be taught by an R.A.C. Registered Instructor who is a Member of the Institute of Advanced Motorists.
You will be taught (with the exception of the Advanced Course) on a 1961 model dual-controlled saloon.

WRITE OR TELEPHONE TO :-
BARRY T. LANGDON
70 WHITLEY COURT ROAD
BIRMINGHAM 32   **WOO 2967**

Remember — " Selfish driving doesn't prove who's right — only who's left ! "

Barrow's

Good Things
for Home
and Kitchen

CORPORATION STREET · BIRMINGHAM

NORMAN GRANZ
&
HAROLD DAVISON

present

AN

EVENING

WITH

ELLA
FITZGERALD

with the Lou Levy Quartet

and

THE
OSCAR
PETERSON
TRIO

Ray Brown · Ed Thigpen

ODEON, NEW STREET
MARCH · 1961

Ella Fitzgerald

Oscar Peterson.

STYLISH PRACTICAL HAIRDRESSING
at moderate prices in the restful, private
cubicles of our new light and airy salon.

Molly Winstone

27 Auchinleck Square
Five Ways

Mid 4758

Alcester Road South, Kings Heath, 1961.

Summer Conference of representatives, display men and depot managers, Cadbury's, 6th June 1961.

BRIGHT JOURNEY

WITH

DOCKERS'
TRANSPORT FINISHES

DOCKER BROTHERS · ROTTON PARK ST · LADYWOOD · BIRMINGHAM
A member of Pinchin Johnson and Associates Limited

APPOINTMENTS SELECTION
(PETER S. FIELDING, B.A., B.S.W.)

SELECTION
EVALUATION
VOCATIONAL
GUIDANCE

32 & 33, Queen's College Chambers
38a PARADISE STREET
BIRMINGHAM, I
Telephones : MIDland 0537-8-9

TECHNICAL, CLERICAL
ADMINISTRATIVE
EXECUTIVE AND
PROFESSIONAL
STAFF.

A FREE AND CONFIDENTIAL SERVICE TO STAFF ! !
MODERATE FEES TO EMPLOYERS
ENQUIRIES — WITHOUT OBLIGATION — ALWAYS WELCOME

Albert Street, 12th June 1961.

Telephone : MIDland 0596

Hair Stylists
Colour Artists

Derek Palmer Ltd

59 John Bright Street

Birmingham. 1

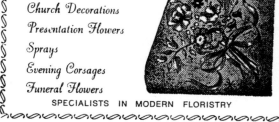

FLOWERS FOR ALL OCCASIONS
by B. G. MITCHELL
270 Alcester Road South, Kings Heath
Ring HIG 1910

Bridal Flowers
Church Decorations
Presentation Flowers
Sprays
Evening Corsages
Funeral Flowers
SPECIALISTS IN MODERN FLORISTRY

Stafford Street/James Watt Street, 1961.

Factory Road/Park Road/Benson Road, Soho, 29th June 1961.

Electro Magnets Ltd., Hampton Street/Bond Street, Newtown, 1961.

The demise of the Crown Inn, Snow Hill/Bath Street, 29th June 1961.

SEAGER (BEARINGS) LTD.

OFFICIAL STOCKISTS OF ALL LEADING MAKES OF

BALL & ROLLER BEARINGS

52-54 GOLDSMITH ROAD, KINGS HEATH, 14

Tel. Highbury 5391 (3 Lines)

N.T. FROST LTD.

Specialist electroplaters of small parts in quantity

SILVER ■ HARD GOLD
NICKEL ■ CHROME
CADMIUM ■ TIN/ZINC
SPECULUM
RHODIUM
VACUUM COATING
BARREL POLISHING

fully approved
WAR OFFICE
M.O.A. and A.R.B.

N.T. FROST LTD.

Harford St.
Birmingham 19
tel. CEN. 4135

The Birmingham & Midland Operatic Society about to start rehearsing for "The King & I", Hippodrome, October 1961. It was their 75th production.

HIPPODROME — BIRMINGHAM

6th NOVEMBER — FOR TWO WEEKS

Williamson Music Ltd. present

A BIG NEW PRODUCTION OF

'OKLAHOMA!'

20th NOVEMBER — FOR THREE WEEKS

THE SMASH-HIT JAZZ MUSICAL

'KING KONG'

from the Princes Theatre, London

PANTOMIME SEASON 1961/62
Commencing Thursday, December 21st, Friday, December 22nd
and Saturday, December 23rd at 7.0 (Closed Xmas Day). Subsequently
7.0   EVENINGS   7.0
MATINEES at 2.30 as below:—
Week Commencing December 25th   ...   Tues., Wed., Thurs., Fri. & Sat.
Week Commencing January 1st ...   ...   Daily
Week Commencing January 8th onwards   Wed., Thurs. & Sat.

TOM ARNOLD & EMILE LITTLER PRESENT

LONNIE DONEGAN

IN

'CINDERELLA'

WITH

3 MONARCHS, AUDREY JEANS, HAYNES & LARUE

Lonnie Donegan.

Harmonica wizards, the 3 Monarchs.   25

Bell Holloway, Northfield, 23rd January 1962.

SUTTON
AND
ASH
LIMITED

BIRMINGHAM 18

IRON AND STEEL STOCKHOLDERS

TELEGRAMS: "ELF, BIRMINGHAM"
TELEPHONE: NORTHERN 2242 (6 lines)

ROUNDS · SQUARES
CHANNELS · JOISTS
FLATS · ANGLES
TEES AND PLATES
IN ALL SIZES

WORKING-UP SHEETS. C.R.C.A.
BLACK AND GALVANIZED

H Humperston & Sons Ltd. (scrap metal merchants), Cherrywood Road,
Bordesley Green, 2nd February 1962.

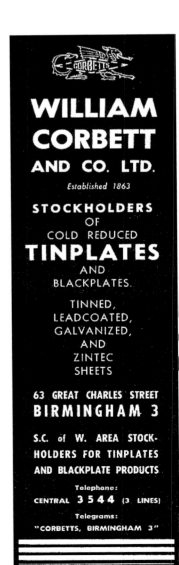

WILLIAM CORBETT AND CO. LTD.
Established 1863

STOCKHOLDERS
OF
COLD REDUCED
TINPLATES
AND
BLACKPLATES.

TINNED,
LEADCOATED,
GALVANIZED,
AND
ZINTEC
SHEETS

63 GREAT CHARLES STREET
BIRMINGHAM 3

S.C. of W. AREA STOCK-
HOLDERS FOR TINPLATES
AND BLACKPLATE PRODUCTS

Telephone:
CENTRAL 3544 (3 LINES)

Telegrams:
"CORBETTS, BIRMINGHAM 3"

HUGHES, LATHBURY LTD.

**SPECIALISTS FOR FINE LIMIT TOOLS.
PRECISION PRESSINGS FOR AIRCRAFT, MOTOR AND
OTHER TRADES, IN STAINLESS STEEL AND ALL METALS**
A.I.D. & A.R.B. APPROVED

105 Hospital Street
BIRMINGHAM 19

Aston Cross 3797-8

"There'll be another bus along soon – won't there?"
Colmore Row, March 1962.

Eric Delaney leads his big band on tympani,
Town Hall, February 1962.

Old Oscott F.C., Handsworth District League, c 1962.

Dudley Road, Winson Green, 1962.

Gordon Teakle braces himself for the rush hour, 1962.

Prefects and sub-prefects, with Headmaster, Major Jolley (light suit) and the Deputy Head, Mr Wickstead, Cockshut Hill School for Boys, Yardley, 1962. Major Jolley had tried to teach Alton (never the brightest of pupils!) at Saltley Grammar School.

St Paul's Roman Catholic Grammar School for Girls, Vernon Road, Edgbaston, March 1962.

King's Norton Grammar School for Boys, Northfield Road, 1962.

A.T.MEAR & CO.

GENERAL PRINTERS and COMMERCIAL STATIONERS

Specialists in one-time carbon sets.

General Office System Printing. Stationery and paper supplies.

90-91 COX STREET WEST, BALSALL HEATH, BIRMINGHAM, 12

Tel. No. Calthorpe 4445

The Crown and Cushion, Birchfield Road, Perry Barr, 3rd April 1962.

CONNOLLY & OLIVIERI, LTD.

80 & 81 NEW STREET	793 HAGLEY ROAD WEST
BIRMINGHAM, 2	QUINTON, 32
Telephone: Midland 3833	Telephone: Woodgate 2012

A SMALL SELECTION FROM OUR LIST OF

RED BORDEAUX

VIN ROUGE DE BORDEAUX
7/6 per bottle
(A pleasant dry wine for drinking at any meal time.)

CHATEAU LA ROSE CAPBERN, 1952
11/6 per bottle
(Worth buying now, and putting away for twelve months.)

CHATEAU PONTET CANET, 1953
14/3 per bottle
(A high quality wine— perfect right now.)

CHATEAU MOUTON ROTHSCHILD, 1934
36/6 per bottle
(Only to be consumed on very special occasions—but what a treat!)

Alum Rock Road, April 1962.

Once in every generation comes a tale of such classic horror that even its terror fascinates...while it holds you forever captive with its frightening power!!!

The Greatest THRILL CLASSIC of All Time!!!

"THE PHANTOM OF THE OPERA"

Eastman COLOR

Starring HERBERT LOM · HEATHER SEARS · also Starring THORLEY WALTERS · MICHAEL GOUGH

Screenplay by JOHN ELDER · Directed by TERENCE FISHER · Produced by ANTHONY HINDS · A Hammer Film Production · A Universal International Release

Washwood Heath Road, Ward End, 18th May 1962.

A maze of fire hoses after a fire at Elcock & Sons Ltd. (metal spinners), Tindal Street, Balsall Heath, 18th May 1962.

Rear of Heneage Street, Nechells, 21st June 1962.

GABRIEL and COMPANY LIMITED

*Manufacturers of all
Stainless Steel Handrails
and
Fittings for Motor Buses*

—

A.B. ROW . BIRMINGHAM, 4

ALOUETTE REGD.

TOURIST REGD.

LARKNIT REGD.

*BRAND NAMES OF DISTINCTION
in the World of Clothing*

S. C. LARKINS & SONS LIMITED
WHOLESALE TEXTILE DISTRIBUTORS
LIVERY STREET . BIRMINGHAM

NO FINER T.V. VALUE ANYWHERE!!

19" T.V. RENTAL

for only

8/3 WEEKLY

WITH "NEVER WITHOUT A SET SERVICE"

B. R. W. RENTALS

**2248 COVENTRY ROAD, SHELDON
BIRMINGHAM 26**

AND BRANCHES THROUGHOUT THE CITY
Telephone SHE 2928

An air-bridge across the Atlantic. That's the Air-India Maharajah service from London to New York. Altogether a delightful concept in Atlantic air travel, at one time reserved for travellers heading East. Demure, sari-clad hostesses. Decor of Indian motifs and fabrics. Select dishes from East or West. And of course Boeing Rolls-Royce jets.

AIR-INDIA

The world's first all-jet airline   Over 30 years of flying experience

Birmingham, Glasgow, Leeds and Manchester.

Mrs Dorothy Cadbury (3rd left)President of Birmingham District Girls' Life Brigade, joins other members for a canal trip from Gas Street Basin, 7th July 1962.

CERTIFICATE OF BAPTISM

Michael Roy Dillon
WAS BAPTIZED AT

Shaw Heath Church: St Margaret, Somerset Road.

on *22 July 1962*   *Birmingham 23*

Priest

This child has begun life as a Christian: it is the duty of the parents and sponsors to see that *he* goes on according to this beginning.

And is

Trained to pray and taught the Christian Faith.
Trained to Christian habits as soon as possible.
Helped to know and understand the Church's Catechism.
Encouraged to attend Church by personal example.
Brought to Confirmation when the Church's Catechism is known and understood.

Early teaching and early training in good habits should lead to early Confirmation. Your Child will then be able to approach God's Altar and receive the Bread of Life. Going out into the World at the end of Childhood, the Child will have formed the habit of prayer and the use of God's holy Sacraments, to give strength in temptation and protection from evil.

Mowbrays 151   *Printed in Great Britain*

Pandora

**5 Sheaf Lane, Sheldon
Birmingham 26**
Telephone SHE 2052

Coats   Gowns
Knitwear   Hosiery
Lingerie   Jewellery

CAMILLE
HAIR STYLIST
SHE 2463 (First Floor)
STYLING
SETTING
TINTING, ETC.

Highgate Stores, Hick Street/Highgate Street, 1962.

Looking across the dark roof of New Street Station, towards the spire of St Philip's, 3rd October 1962.

Corporation Street, 12th January 1963.

Easy Row/Edmund Street, 30th January 1963.

The beginning of the end of parts of Bath Street, 30th January 1963.

Clapgate Lane/Woodgate Lane, Woodgate, 1963.

The new Crescent Theatre starts to take shape, Cumberland Street, 29th October 1963. It opened twelve months later.

CINEPHONE
CONTINENTAL CINEMA
BRISTOL STREET --- MID 1761

STILL SHOWING, THE FILM THAT HIT THE HEADLINES

The Yellow Teddybears 'X'

Starring Annette Whiteley and the new beat group The Embers.

Also

Thrills . . . Chills . . . Nerve racking Suspense
THE TERROR OF DR. HICHCOCK (x)
(Technicolor)

LAST COMPLETE PROGRAMME 7.35

TOWN HALL, BIRMINGHAM
NEW YEAR'S EVE TWITCH

Twitch and Twist the New Year in with

Johnny Neal and The Starliners
Roy Everett and The Climbers
Johnny King and The Diamonds
The Sidewinders

ADMISSION 10/-   8 p.m. - 1 a.m.   Licensed Bar
Tickets available at Town Hall Box Office.

TOWN HALL — BIRMINGHAM
GARY PROMOTIONS (Birmingham) Present

JOHNNY KIDD   GENE VINCENT
AND THE PIRATES

& HEINZ
with—from LIVERPOOL

WAYNE FONTANA and the MINDBENDERS
from BIRMINGHAM

THE ROCKIN' BERRIES
on

THURSDAY, DECEMBER 12 at 6.30 & 8.45 p.m.

TICKETS: 10/6, 8/6, 6/6, 4/-
from Town Hall Box Office (CEN 2392) and Usual Agents

CITY OF BIRMINGHAM SYMPHONY ORCHESTRA
TOWN HALL, BIRMINGHAM

THURSDAY, DECEMBER 19, at 7.30 p.m. TONIGHT

CHRISTMAS CONCERT
Conductor: HAROLD GRAY

Overture, Hansel and Gretel	Humperdink
Hark The Herald Angels Sing	
It Came Upon The Midnight Clear	
Peter and The Wolf	Prokofiev
Soirées Musicales	Rossini/Britten
Away In A Manger	
Christmas Oratorio (Excerpts)	Bach
Vltava	Smetana
O Come All Ye Faithful	

BIRMINGHAM CHORAL UNION

TICKETS: 8/6 to 2/6   CEN 2392

Booking: TOWN HALL BOX OFFICE

TOWN HALL, BIRMINGHAM
Friday, January 3, 1964, at 7 p.m.

A CONCERT OF SEASONAL MUSIC
by

DR. GEORGE THALBEN-BALL (CITY ORGANIST)
and

THE TEMPLARS MALE CHOIR
with

BOY CHORISTERS OF THE TEMPLE CHURCH

ADMISSION FREE

The Rev Geoffrey Brown with some of the children who attended the Christmas Party, Teviot Tower, Mosborough Crescent, Hockley, 1963.

KEN SEDGLEY
MOTOR CYCLES

SALES — SPARES — REPAIRS
Main Agents for:
Greeves : Ariel : B.S.A. : Honda & Suzuki
Raleigh

New 1964 Models in Stock for Immediate Delivery

1956 JAMES Captain	£30
1956 VESPA 125	£35
1958 VESPA 150 G.S.	£45
1961 CAPRI 80 c.c.	£45
1962 CAPRI 80 c.c.	£65
1958 JAMES 250	£65
1959 B.S.A. 500 Shooting Star	£79
1961 TRIUMPH Tigress 175 c.c.	£79
1961 GREEVES 250 Scrambler	£85
1960 TRIUMPH 350 c.c. T21	£99

Ken Sedgeley   ★

1195 BRISTOL ROAD SOUTH
NORTHFIELD, BIRMINGHAM

Just a few of the Used Bargains in Stock

TEL.: PRI 1559

CHRISTMAS SHOPPING

Watch Out!
IT'S GETTING LATE!

For
TOYS
and Fishing Tackle
D. A. THOMAS
209 Station Road, Stechford
STE 2104

CARPETS FOR CHRISTMAS

BAILEY & REYNOLDS
Fitted carpet specialists
Free fitting
Free underlay
196 Washwood Heath Rd.
Birmingham 8

Special Night Service
Monday to Friday
6.30 p.m. - 9.30 p.m.
Saturday 10 a.m. - 6 p.m.
RING: EAS 2783

1964

Odeon, January 1964.

HELEN FORREST

SAM DONAHUE leader of the TOMMY DORSEY ORCHESTRA

FRANK SINATRA JNR.

Harborne Lane, Selly Oak, 26th February 1964.

MECCA DANCING
GAY TOWER, RESERVOIR ROAD EDGBASTON

General Manager: A. D. BACCIOCHI.   EDG. 0107

Presents your Dancing Programme for the Week

MONDAY: Off The Record Session 7-11 p.m. 2/-
TUESDAY: Gift Night (General Dancing)
7.30-11.30 p.m. 2/6
WEDNESDAY: Over 21 Night, 7.30-11.30 p.m. 3/-
THURSDAY: Big Beat Night 7-11 p.m. 2/-
FRIDAY: Private Party Night (Details from Manager)
SATURDAY: Palais Night, 7.30-11.45 p.m., 5/-
SUNDAY: Sunday Spectacular 7-11 p.m.

Members 2/6, Guests 3/-

AFTERNOONS

WEDNESDAY: Off the Record 3-5 p.m. 1/-
SATURDAY: Beat for the In-Betweens 3-5 p.m. 1/6
SUNDAY: Off the Record 3-5 p.m.

Members 1/6, Guests 2/-

MORNINGS

SATURDAY: Junior Disc Session 12-2 p.m. 1/-

BRIAN PEARSALL AND HIS MUSIC and THE TED POOLE TRIO

Ballroom available every Afternoon except Saturday and Sunday for Conferences, Exhibitions, etc. For details contact Manager.

THORNE BROTHERS
(Members of the National Federation of Master Painters and Decorators of England and Wales)

128 WESTRIDGE ROAD, KINGS HEATH BIRMINGHAM 14

undertake all types of high class

PAINTING & DECORATING

FOR PERSONAL ATTENTION TELEPHONE - SPR 4796

THE NAZZ
THE GROUP FOR EVERY OCCASION

Contact :
Mr. K. Shaw, 8, Chale Grove,
Kings Heath, Birmingham 14
Tel : 475 - 2654

THE LEVY RAMBLERS

Phone :

KIN 5233
ERD 6326

NEW STREET STATION

Phone: CAS 6733. Mr. D. Lloyd
Management: Mr. T. R. BOWN
39, KITTS GREEN ROAD,
KITTS GREEN,
BIRMINGHAM, 33.

THE LYMIES RHYTHM GROUP
Have the Sound YOU Want

BILL MALLARD,
384, Rotton Park Road,
EDGBASTON
Birmingham 16
Phone: SME 3323 (Manager)

JONES & LLOYD Estd. 1933
(RADIO ELECTRICAL LTD)

RENT BUSH or MURPHY T/v

10/6 per week   Statutory Deposit £6-16-6

READY FOR B.B.C.2

907 WALSALL RD. GRE 1824
155 LOZELLS RD. NOR 1802

BBC 2 started on 20th April 1964. Due to a power failure the first two and a half minutes were broadcast in complete silence!

GIFTS
for EASTER at the BULL RING CENTRE

LOOKING for a shopping spree without having to worry about dodging the traffic or moving from one part of the city to another, you can visit one of the most modern market centres in Britain today—the Bull Ring Centre Market.

For the first time, you can board a bus to the centre, to shop in comfort and return to the local bus stop completely under cover.

A principal factor in the development of the project has been the aim to pre- serve the unique atmosphere of a successful retail market and in the Bull Ring Centre Market there is a wide var- iety of trading. In fact, you can possibly purchase any- thing from a pin to a steam roller.

The Bull Ring Centre Market has over 200 stalls and nowhere in the world can you meet a more friend- lier person than these mar- ket stallholders.

Spend a day at the market and you will be delighted and above all save money.

FST Electronic Consultants Ltd
MANUFACTURERS OF ELECTRONIC EQUIPMENT • UPPER PORTLAND STREET, BIRMINGHAM 6
AND CLOSED CIRCUIT TELEVISION TELEPHONE: EAST 0227-8

The band of The Royal Warwickshire Fusiliers plays at the ceremony as a train is named after their regiment, Snow Hill Station, 22nd May 1964.

Queen's Drive and New Street Station undergo extensive alterations, May 1964.

Watching Erdington Round Table's first carnival procession, High Street, Erdington, May 1964.

Quinton British Legion Parade, from World's End Lane to the Parish Church, marking their second anniversary, 28th May 1964.

"Get your fresh fruit & veg here!", Bull Ring, 1964.

The crowds wait to see the Duke of Edinburgh start his day at the Council House, before going on to open the Bull Ring Shopping Centre, 29th May 1964.

CINE-EQUIPMENTS LTD.

EVERYTHING · PHOTOGRAPHIC

CAMERA
GIFT
OUTFITS

make ideal birthday
presents Beautifully
packed in presentation
box.
Our prices from £4-9-3

35 COLMORE ROW
BIRMINGHAM.

Tel:
236
3907

Also at Solihull, Stratford-on-Avon

Senior citizens, from Newtown, about to set off for a day trip to London, June 1964.

Senior citizens leave the Baldwin Inn, Baldwins Lane, Hall Green,
for a trip to Weston-Super-Mare, 1964.

Lea Hall British Legion in their Annual Parade,
13th June 1964.

Ann Saunders (centre) becomes Moseley Round Table's
Carnival Queen. Her attendants are Brenda
Gutteridge and Gillian Lilley, 23rd July 1964.

45

Bristol Road South, Northfield, 1st September 1964.

Farm Street, Hockley, 17th September 1964.

these
famous
makes
await your
inspection
at our
showrooms

Daimler

PJ EVANS

81 - 91 JOHN BRIGHT STREET · BIRMINGHAM 1.   TEL : MID 2911.
and at 10 BIRMINGHAM ROAD, SUTTON COLDFIELD.   TEL : SUT 1920.

Hall Green Cricket Eleven, 1964.

Telephone: EAS. 2087 & 3267

EMAT ENGINEERING LTD.

Manufacturers of PRESS TOOLS, JIGS and FIXTURES   ✦   All Types of General Machining

215 TAME ROAD, WITTON, BIRMINGHAM 6

Alexandra Street, off Shakespeare Road, 24th September 1964. Today the street has completely disappeared.

Edward Road, Balsall Heath, 20th October 1964.

Highfield Road, Hall Green, October 1964.

Bordesley Green Road, November 1964.

Mick Jagger and Petula Clark during a break in recording "Thank Your Lucky Stars", ABC TV Studios, Aston, 28th November 1964.

Owen Street/Wheeleys Lane, Edgbaston, 1964.

High Street, approaching Bull Street and Dale End, 5th January 1965.

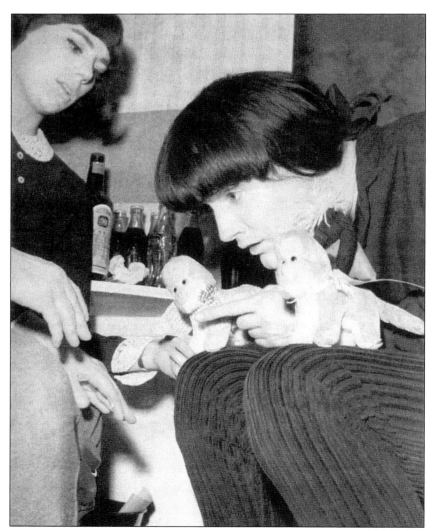

Pop star, P J Proby, in the city to record ABC Television's "Lucky Stars", checks his lucky mascots, 14th January 1965. His record of "Somewhere" was in the charts at the time.

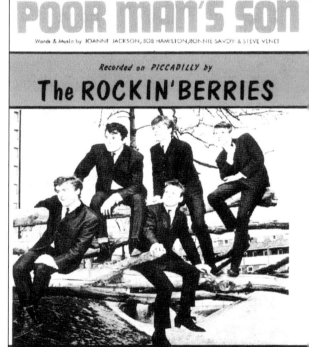

ah!

Allowing for regional variations, this is a word you will always hear on placing Marsh & Baxter pork sausages, pies, bacon or ham before a knowledgeable eater. Technically it is called 'flavour anticipation'. Colloquially it's known as drooling. Marsh & Baxter products are the finest you can buy, and are renowned for their special flavour. Try some on your family. See how quickly the Ah! becomes Mmmm!

MARSH & BAXTER LTD., BRIERLEY HILL & CASTLE BROMWICH

THE
Hippodrome

BIRMINGHAM
Telephone: MID 2576/7

Proprietors: MOSS' EMPIRES LIMITED
Chairman: PRINCE LITTLER, C.B.E.
Managing Director: LESLIE A. MACDONNELL, O.B.E.
Artistes Booking Control .. CISSIE WILLIAMS   *Advertising Manager* .. A. A. COOMBS
Area Supervisor .. .. .. R. S. SWIFT   *Press Representative:* .. JOHN NEIMAN
Musical Supervisor .. .. ERIC TANN   *Chief of Production Dept.* PETER PENROSE
MANAGER and LICENSEE WILFRED MAY   *ASSISTANT MANAGER* .. B. HOPSON

✿✿✿✿✿✿✿✿✿✿✿✿✿✿✿✿✿✿✿✿✿✿✿✿✿✿✿✿

FOR TWO WEEKS. Commencing MONDAY, MARCH 15th, 1965
EVENINGS at 7.15   MATINEE SATURDAY, MARCH 27th ONLY at 2.30

The Birmingham and Midland Operatic Society

PRESENTS *(by arrangement with Samuel French Ltd.)*

THE SPECTACULAR MUSICAL ROMANCE

" KING'S RHAPSODY "

Devised, Written and Composed by
IVOR NOVELLO

Lyrics by Christopher Hassall

✿✿✿✿✿✿✿✿✿✿✿✿✿✿✿✿✿✿✿✿✿✿✿✿✿✿✿✿✿✿✿✿✿✿

Souvenir Programme 1/-

In Aid of National and Local Charities

The Edmund Day Nursery, Edmund Road,
Saltley, 1965.

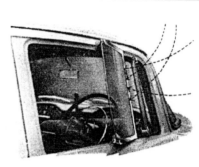

Auster
LTD
Established 1941

NEW STYLE
auxiliary
wings

The Auster Auxiliary Wing, Type Illustrated No. 2000. Fresh air without draught.

Also available smart Exterior Hood Visors for complete protection from dazzle.

AUSTER LIMITED
Crown Works, Barford Street, Birmingham 5

Parade, between Edward Street and Summer Row, 1965.

51

The view from the Rotunda, with Moor Street Station on the right, 1965.

The "Sir Nigel Gresley" pulls in to Snow Hill Station, 24th March 1965.

PLUMBING AND	**GENERAL CONTRACTOR**	MODERN GRATES
ZINC WORK Etc.	**FOR DECORATIONS**	SINKS & LAVATORIES
ESTIMATES	**PROPERTY REPAIRS & ALTERATIONS**	SUPPLIED & FIXED
FREE		CENTRAL HEATING

FREDERICK ROE

Tel. VIC 4541

184 PRETORIA ROAD · BORDESLEY GREEN · BIRMINGHAM 9

M r.D.Manton,3A,Solihull Lane,Birmingham.   31st March 196 5.

Staircase redecorated to suit.
Supplying and fitting Gas Pipe to suit.

Materials.

12 pieces 1395 @ 8/6.	5.	2.	–					
less 20% discount.	1.	–	4					
	4.	1.	8					
plus pur.tax.		4.	1					
14 lbs.Distemper.				4.	5.	9		
1 length ½ Gas Pipe.					18.	–		
1 ½" Elbow x M.I.				1.	5.	4		
6– ½" Elbows.						9		
2– ½" TEES. ¼" Centre.					3.	6		
2 Pipe Hooks. 2 Nipples (Spacing).					1.	8		
					2.	–		
Labour.				6.	17.	–		
				8.	10.	–		
Total.	£	15.	7.	–				

Paid with thanks
F. Roe

GEORGE ROBINSON
F.A.I.

CHARTERED
AUCTIONEERS
&
ESTATE AGENTS
SURVEYORS
& VALUERS

RATING
CONSULTANTS

1 NEWHALL STREET
BIRMINGHAM · 3
Central 0272 (Two Lines)

ALSO AT

30 BORE STREET
LICHFIELD
STAFFORDSHIRE
Lichfield 2958 (Three Lines)

FGF
(ASTON) LTD.

THE ASBESTOS AND
LAGGING SPECIALISTS.
MILLBOARDS, CLOTHS, YARNS, TAPES,
JOINTS, PACKINGS, SHEETS, FLUE PIPE,
ASBESTOS CEMENT GOODS ETC.
LARGE STOCKS ALWAYS AVAILABLE.
CAN QUOTE FOR CUT SIZES.

PRINCIP ST.,BIRMINGHAM,4.
TEL. 021-359 3925.
TELE. 33 8596.

Lesbrook Limited

PRESSINGS
IN ALL
METALS

ICKNIELD
SQUARE, 16
PHONE: EDGBASTON
0962 · 3 · 4
GRAMS: "INTENSIVE
B'HAM, 16."
Nº 2 WORKS :
PORT ST. EVESHAM
Nº 3 WORKS :
PARKFIELD ROAD
BIRMINGHAM, 8

DOUGLAS
SMALLWOOD
& CO. F.A.I.

Chartered
Auctioneers &
Estate Agents
Valuers, Surveyors,
Factory & Machinery
Specialists

GRIFFIN HOUSE
18-19 LUDGATE HILL 3
TELEPHONE
CENTRAL 5921/2

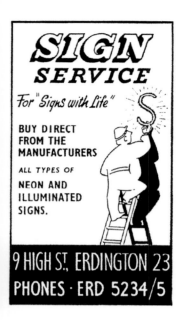

SIGN SERVICE

For "Signs with Life"

BUY DIRECT FROM THE MANUFACTURERS

ALL TYPES OF **NEON** AND **ILLUMINATED SIGNS**.

9 HIGH ST. ERDINGTON 23

PHONES · ERD 5234/5

Steam Traction Engine Rally, Newhall Street, c 1965.

C.H.MILLER (ENGINEERS) LTD.

24/26 ALBERT RD. ASTON·6

Stockists BOLTS · NUTS · SCREWS · WASHERS · ETC. ENGINEERS STUDS · SOCKET HEAD CAP & SET SCREWS.

PHONE: NORTHERN 9371 (5 LINES)

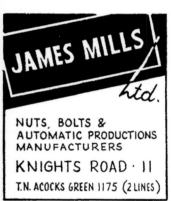

JAMES MILLS ltd.

NUTS, BOLTS & AUTOMATIC PRODUCTIONS MANUFACTURERS

KNIGHTS ROAD · 11

T.N. ACOCKS GREEN 1175 (2 LINES)

Holloway Head/Marshall Street, 1965.

F.W. Rednall and Sons

ESTABLISHED OVER 50 YEARS

HOUSE LAND & ESTATE AGENTS

BROADFIELD CHAMBERS 150, SUTTON ROAD ERDINGTON 23 PHONE·ERDINGTON·0437

Lichfield Road, Aston, 1965.

Pershore Road, Stirchley, 3rd August 1965.

Palmerston Road, Sparkbrook, 1965.

BUY YOUR WOOD WOOL FROM THE ACTUAL MANUFACTURERS

BIRMINGHAM WOOD WOOL LTD.

BALES   PACKING CASE MAKERS   PADS

418-422 MOSELEY ROAD BIRMINGHAM 12   Phone   Calthorpe 1538 (5 LINES)

Washington Street/Upper Gough Street, 3rd August 1965.

Barford Street, 3rd August 1965.

Kyotts Lake Road, Sparkbrook, 1965.

A DEBENHAM STORE

SALE OF THE MIDLANDS GREYS

WONDERFUL WEEK-END BARGAINS

9 a.m. SCOOPS
Personal Shoppers Only

EXTRA! GIGANTIC WEEKEND
FASHION CLEARANCE!

15 Only 3ft. DIVAN SET
Complete Each £7-19-6

1 only LOUNGE SUITE
NOW £15

1 only SINK UNIT
NOW 55/-

30 only SUITCASES
NOW 10/-

10 only
24-pce. DINNER SERVICES
NOW 45/-

24 only BATH TOWELS
NOW 2/6

TWEED HOLIDAY COATS
NOW £6-19-11

COATS IN TWEEDS AND PASTELS
NOW all at each £6

PHILIP KUNICK TOPSIZE
NOW £5-19-11

JERSEY JUMPER SUITS
NOW 59/11

YOUNG STYLE DRESSES
NOW 29/11

CORDUROY RAINCOATS
NOW £5-5-0

SHOWERPROOF POPLINS
NOW 79/11

NYLON RAINCOATS
NOW 45/-

WATERPROOF RAINCOATS
NOW 39/11

LADIES' BLOUSES
NOW 12/11

LONDON MAID SKIRTS
NOW 19/11

STRETCH SLACKS
NOW 19/11

Ladies' Assorted KNITWEAR
NOW 19/11

ALEXANDRA THEATRE

IN ASSOCIATION WITH

THE CITY OF BIRMINGHAM
FESTIVAL OF ENTERTAINMENTS

FORWARD

MAIGRET AND THE LADY

SEPTEMBER 6th — SEPTEMBER 11th 1965

Programme : Sixpence

TYPEWRITER AND ACCOUNTING MACHINE SERVICES

| ACCOUNTING MACHINES | ADDING MACHINES | CALCULATING MACHINES |
| TYPEWRITERS | PORTABLES | FURNITURE & SUPPLIES |

LEE BANK HOUSE, HOLLOWAY HEAD, BIRMINGHAM I
Telephone MIDland 6563

Twinlock SYSTEMS

Chamberlain Square, with the Central Library on the left, 1965.

Alum Rock Road, with Ellesmere Road just in view on the right, Saltley, 1965.

Dymoke Street/Angelina Street, Highgate, October 1965.

Stephenson Place/New Street, 13th October 1965.

Rear of Great Russell Street, Newtown, 15th November 1965.

The dispute with the Bakers Union caused many city shops a few headaches, 19th November 1965.

JOHN DYER, F.V.I.

Estate Agent
Valuer
Auctioneer and
Surveyor

Telephone: MIDland 5347
DISTRICT BANK CHAMBERS, 24 BENNETTS HILL
BIRMINGHAM 2

Hotels Register

BIRMINGHAM HOTELS in the City Centre

NAME AND ADDRESS	TEL. NO.	LICENSED OR UNLICENSED	NO. OF BEDROOMS	BED AND BREAKFAST
*§ ALBANY HOTEL, Smallbrook Ringway, 5	MIDland 8171	L	250	†72/6
*§ ARDEN HOTEL, New Street, 5	MIDland 1029	U	100	From 28/-
BLACK SWAN HOTEL, Bromsgrove Street, 5	MIDland 3566	L	20	From 25/-
*§ GRAND HOTEL, Colmore Row, 3	CENtral 7301	L	200	From 52/6
* IMPERIAL HOTEL, Temple Street, 2	MIDland 6751	L	78	40/-
MARKET HOTEL, Station Street, 5	MIDland 1134	L	38	35/-
* MIDLAND HOTEL, New Street, 2	MIDland 2601	L	133	52/6
§ NEW VICTORIA HOTEL, 34 Corporation Street, 2	MIDland 5313	L	60	37/6
* QUEEN'S HOTEL, Stephenson Place, 2	MIDland 4433	L	168	From 47/6
§ WAVERLEY HOTEL, New Meeting Street, 4	MIDland 0634	L	25	25/-

Information concerning the establishments listed is furnished by the proprietors and inclusion here does not imply any form of recommendation. Charges shown were correct at the time of going to press but are subject to alteration without notice. Intending visitors are advised to make their reservations as early as possible and to confirm that the charges shown still apply.

REFERENCE MARKS: * Joint Appointment RAC, AA, RSAC.
§ Member of the Birmingham and District Hotels and Restaurants Association.

A LIST of HOTELS and PRIVATE HOTELS, not in the City Centre, is available from the City of Birmingham's Information Department at the Council House, Birmingham, 1. Telephone: CENtral 9944.

A visitor requiring accommodation in Birmingham may call "Phon-O-Tel" Ltd., ACOcks Green 5858 and be informed which hotels have vacancies. This is a free service sponsored by the Hotel Industry to assist the visitor.

Not forgetting the smaller hotels - Alcester Lodge Hotel, Alcester Road, Moseley, 28th January 1966.

N. J. LOVETT & CO. LTD.
(SUCCESSORS TO LEONARD PROCTER LTD.)

WELDING ENGINEERS
SPECIALISING IN REPAIRS
Cast Iron, Aluminium and Aluminium Alloys

TELEPHONE: VIC. 0457
81 & 83 KYRWICKS LANE
SPARKBROOK
BIRMINGHAM - 11

Gravelly Hill/Slade Road, Erdington, 1966.

Chester Road, Pype Hayes, 4th February 1966.

the sheer elegance of

Rembrandt

is now at
Lewis's

A dress that wears
its best bib tucked.
Topped by
matching jacket.
Both in Barbicans.
Style 282. Sizes
10-20. Also short
fittings. 10½ gns.

LEWIS'S

have a *flair* for fashion

B.151   LEWIS'S LTD., BIRMINGHAM, 4. Tel.: CEN. 8251

Famous—name knitwear
at Lewis's....

Donbros

Easy-care 'Crimplene' cardigan with raglan sleeves in
white, blue, turquoise, pink, beige or lemon.
36in. **54/11** 38in. **57/6** 40in. **59/11**
second floor

LEWIS'S

have a *flair* for fashion

B.152   LEWIS'S LTD., BIRMINGHAM, 4. Tel.: CEN. 8251

Hawkesley Farm Moat Estate, 1966.

EXPERT
EAR PIERCING

by appointment at

PERRY GREAVES

GOLDSMITHS & JEWELLERS
Colmore Circus (opp. Gaumont Cinema)
Fee 3 gns. Inclusive of modern Gold Sleepers
Telephone: CENtral 9297

H.B.SALE LTD

ESTABLISHED 1860

NAME PLATES IN BRONZE
BRASS & PLASTIC
INCLUDING
INSTRUCTION & SERIAL NAME
PLATES, PRESSED
ENGRAVED & PRINTED

PROGRESS WORKS, SUMMER LANE,
SNOW HILL, BIRMINGHAM · 19
Tel. CENTRAL 5661

WE ARE THE CARPET CLEANERS
with three generations experience

Persian
Wilton
Axminster
Chinese
Fitted Carpets

ALSO
CURTAINS
—
LOOSE
COVERS
etc.
expertly
cleaned
&
dyed.
—
FAST
ON SITE
CLEANING
—

FREE COLLECTION IN THE
MIDLANDS AREA
PATENT STEAM
CARPET CLEANING CO. LTD.

2336/8 COVENTRY RD.
SHELDON

SHE 6060

AUSTIN

TOP VALUE IN USED CARS
E & K

1963 Model AUSTIN A40 Mk. II de luxe saloon £465
1962 AUSTIN A110 de luxe overdrive saloon £830
1963 AUSTIN A.35 Mk II Van £295
1963 AUSTIN A60 de luxe saloon £610
1961 VANDEN PLAS 3-Litre automatic saloon £700
1963 AUSTIN MINI SUPER de luxe saloon £420
1961 AUSTIN A40 de luxe saloon £370
1962 VAUXHALL CRESTA saloon £545
1963 AUSTIN A40 Mk II de luxe saloon £495
1963 AUSTIN A40 Mk II de luxe countryman £495
1963 AUSTIN MINI VAN £295
1963 FORD ANGLIA de luxe saloon £435
1962 FORD ZODIAC Mk III saloon £715
1962 AUSTIN MINI de luxe saloon £345
1959 AUSTIN A40 de luxe saloon £270
1959 Model SINGER GAZELLE saloon £325
1962 RILEY 4 72 de luxe saloon £595

EVANS & KITCHEN

HORSEFAIR AND HURST STREET, BIRMINGHAM 1
MID 2781

free car park is in Thorp Street

BARCLAYS

NEW BRANCH

A new branch is now open at

449 Stratford Road, Sparkbrook,
Birmingham 11

Telephone : VICtoria 4985

The hours of business are Mondays to Fridays from
10 a.m. to 3 p.m. Saturdays from 9 a.m. to 11.30
a.m. The Manager, Mr. J. R. Morgan, will welcome the
opportunity of meeting you and showing you the new
premises. Why not call and find out for yourself how
useful an account with Barclays can be to you ?

Barclays Bank
Money is our business

Washwood Heath Road, Ward End, 6th May 1966.

Lingard Street, Nechells, 6th May 1966.

ESTD. 1889

C.H.TAYLOR & CO. LTD.

Manufacturers of

BRIGHT STEEL BARS

ROUNDS	SQUARES	HEX	FLATS
UP TO 10" DIA.	UP TO 3½" SQ	UP TO 3½" A/F	UP TO 12" x 2"

BRIGHT MILD STEEL
FREECUTTING & LEADED STEELS
BLACK MILD, CARBON
and ALLOY STEELS
Precision Cut Blanks to Customers'
Tolerances, Flame Cuttings
Stainless Steels
Forgings

For unrivalled service ring

C. H. TAYLOR & CO. LTD.

DARTMOUTH STREET
ASTON CROSS
BIRMINGHAM 7
ASTON CROSS 4447-8-9

Dartmouth Street/Chester Street, Aston Cross, 3rd June 1966.

The happiest way to go places —
A flying start to your carefree holiday

GREATEST FACILITIES — CHEAPEST FARE
FLY ALL OVER THE WORLD
CAR HIRE SERVICE, HOTEL RESERVATION, RAIL BOOKING
VISAS AND PASSPORTS ARRANGED IMMEDIATELY
FOR YOUR HOLIDAY

PLEASE RING

OR CONTACT —

11 Dawson Road, Handsworth,
Birmingham, 21.
Telephone: NORTHERN 2496

WORLDWAY TRAVEL CENTRE

DAY, NIGHT, FIRST OR TOURIST CLASS FLIGHTS —
TRAVEL CREDIT FACILITIES AVAILABLE

Rear of The Saracen's Head, The Green, Kings Norton,
20th June 1966.

AT YOUR LOCAL CINEMAS
* Denotes six-day programme.

ACOCKS GREEN, Warwick.—
ACO. 0766.—Jean Seberg, Honor
Blackman, "Moment to Moment" (A).
1.25, 4.45, 8.25. "Doctor in Love" (A).
3.5, 6.35. Sun. "Modesty Blaise" (A).

ASTON. ABC.—"The Revenge
of Spartacus" (U), 2.0, 5.25, 8.45.
"Man from Bitter Ridge" (U), 3.40, 7.5.
Sun. "Attila the Hun" (U).

DUDLEY ROAD. Grove. —
Elvis Presley, "Frankie & Johnny"
(U), 3.0, 6.0, 8.55, "Swingin' Set" (U), 1.35,
4.30, 7.30. Sun. "Night Holds Terror" (A).

EDGBASTON. ABC Picture
House.—Norman Wisdom, "Follow
a Star" (U), 1.10, 4.55, 8.45. "Doctor at
Sea" (U). L.P. 6.40.

ERDINGTON. ABC Palace.—
"Frankie & Johnny" (U), 2.15, 5.35,
9.0. "Swingin' Set" (U), 3.45, 7.10. Sun.
"List of Adrian Messenger" (A).

GREAT BARR. Beacon. —
"A Patch of Blue" (A), 4.55, 8.35
(Sat. 1.20). "Made in Paris" (A), 6.45
(Sat. 3.5). Sun. "Moment to Moment" (A).

HALL GREEN. ABC Robin
Hood.—Sidney Poitier, "A Patch of
Blue" (A), 1.5, 4.55, 8.45. "Made in
Paris" (A), 2.55, 6.45. Sun. "Wizard of
Baghdad" (u).

HANDSWORTH. ABC. —
Sidney Poitier, "A PATCH OF
BLUE" (A), 1.10, 4.55, 8.40. "Made in
Paris" (A). L.P. 6.40. Son.: "S.O.S.
Pacific" (A).

HANDSWORTH. Villa Cross.
NOR. 0607.—Yul Brynner, "Taras
Bulba" (U), 4.35, 8.25. "Gunfight at
Dodge City" (U), 2.50, 6.40. Doors open
2.40 (Fri. d.o. 4.30). S. "McLintock" (A).

HAY MILLS. ABC Adelphi.—
"A Patch of Blue" (A), 4.50, 8.40
Sat. 1.0. "Made in Paris" (A). L.P. 6.40.
Sun.: "List of Adrian Messenger" (A).

KING'S HEATH. Kingsway.—
Dirk Bogarde, "Darling" (x), 4.8,
8.10. "Please Turn Over" (A), 2.25, 6.20.
L.P. 6.20. Sun: "Modesty Blaise" (A).

KING'S NORTON. KIN. 1079.
"Frankie & Johnny" (U), 2.30,
5.15, 8.40. "The Swingin' Set" (U),
L.P. 7.5 Sun.:

LONGBRIDGE. Essoldo. PRI.
2470.—"Frankie & Johnny" (U) 2.26,
5.17, 8.13. "Swingin' Set" (U). L.P. 7.23
(No Mat. Fri., Sat.) S.: Modesty Blaise (A).

MOSELEY ROAD. ABC. Cont.
2.45 (Fri.) 4.20 "A Patch of Blue"
(A) 4.45, 8.30. "Made in Paris" (A) 2.45,
6.30. Sun.:

OLTON. Cinema. Aco. 0593.
"A Patch of Blue" (A) 5.0, 8.35.
"Made in Paris" (A) 6.45 (Sat 3.10). S.:
"Inside Daisy Clover" (x).

PERRY BARR. Clifton. —
"Our Man Flint" (U) 5.31, 8.42 (Sat.
2.50). "The Earth Dies Screaming" (A)
7.20 (S. 4.19). S. "Thief of Baghdad" (U).

PERRY BARR. Odeon. Cont.
2.5 Elvis Presley "FRANKIE AND
JOHNNY" (U) 2.20, 5.50, 9.0. "THE
SWINGIN' SET" (U) 3.45, 7.20 Sun. —
"MODESTY BLAISE" (A).

QUINTON. Essoldo. — Elvis
Presley "Frankie & Johnny" (U) 2.30,
5.50, 9.10. "The Swingin Set" (U) 4.0,
7.20 (No Mat Fri.) Sun.:

SALTLEY. Rock. Eas. 0476.—
Elvis Presley "FRANKIE AND
JOHNNY" (u), 5.10, 8.55 (Sat 4.55, 8.45).
"McLintock" (U). L.P. 6.40 (Sat. 6.30).
Sun.: "Cape Fear" (x).

SELLY OAK. ABC Oak. —
Elvis Presley "FRANKIE &
JOHNNY" (U) 2.0, 5.30, 8.55, "SWINGIN'
SET" (U) 3.35, 7.0 Sun?

SHELDON. — Elvis Presley
"Frankie & Johnny" (U) (2.10 Sat.),
5.30, 8.55, "Kings of the Sun" (u) (3.35 S.),
7.0. Sun. "Legion's Last Patrol" (A).

SHIRLEY. Odeon. SHI. 1183.—
Elvis Presley "FRANKIE &
JOHNNY" (U) 2.10, 5.35, 9.0. "THE
SWINGIN' SET" (U) 3.45, 7.10 (No Mat.
Fr. D.O. 5.10). Sun. "Modesty Blaise" (A).

SMALL HEATH. Kingston. —
"Frankie & Johnny" (u), 5.40, 8.50
(Sat. 2.20). "Kings of the Sun" (U) 7.5 (S.
3.45). Sun. "Wild and the Willing" (x).

SMETHWICK. Princes. SME.
0221.—Yul Brynner, "The Magnificent
Seven" (U), 5.35, 8.25 (Th. Sat. 2.50).
Supp. Sun.: "Our Man in Marrakesh" (A).

SOLIHULL. Cinema. SOL. 0398.
Dean Martin, Stella Stevens "THE
SILENCERS" (A) 5.16, 8.38. "BROKEN
SABRE" (U), 7.0 Matinee Sat. 1.55. "
Darling" (x).

SPARKBROOK. ABC.—Elvis
Presley, "Frankie & Johnny" (U),
2.5, 5.30, 8.50, "Swingin' Set" (U), 3.35,
7.0. Sun. "The Bridge" (A).

SPARKBROOK. Waldorf. —
Jerry Lewis, "The Family Jewels"
(u), Dana Andrews, "Town Tamer" (A).
Sun. "Guns of the Black Witch" (A).

STIRCHLEY. ABC Cine-Bowl.
Frank Sinatra, "Von Ryans Express"
(U), 4.25, 8.25. "Apache Rifles" (U), 2.30,
6.25. Sun. "Blind Date" (A).

STOCKLAND GREEN. Plaza.
Sidney Poitier, "A Patch of Blue"
(A), 5.16, 8.46 (Sat. 2.0). "Made in Paris"
(A), 7.5. Sun. "Inside Daisy Clover" (x).

SUTTON COLDFIELD. ABC.—
"A Patch of Blue" (A), 1.5, 4.50,
8.35. "Made in Paris" (A), 2.55, 6.40.
Sun. "The Criminal" (x).

SUTTON COLDFIELD. Odeon.
Elvis Presley, "Frankie & Johnny"
(U), 2.5, 5.30, 8.50, Nancy Sinatra, "The
Swingin' Set" (U), 3.35, 7.0. Sun.
"Modesty Blaise" (U).

WARD END. Beaufort. —
Elvis Presley, "Frankie & Johnny"
(U), John Wayne, "McLintock" (U), L.P.
6.23. Sun. "Seven Ways from Sundown" (A).

WARD END. Capitol. — "A
Patch of Blue" (A), 5.0, 8.35, "Made
in Paris" (A), 6.45 (Sat. 3.10). Sun.
"Inside Daisy Clover" (x).

ALDRIDGE CINEMA

AVION. ALDRIDGE 52312.—
"That Riviera Touch", 5.13, 8.31,
(Sat. 1.55), "Lively Set" (U), 6.51 (Sat.
3.33). Sun. "The Girl Rosemarie" (x).

HALESOWEN CINEMA

LYTTLETON. HAL. 1448. —
"Great St. Trinians Train
Robbery" (U), 5.25, 8.30, "Torpedo Bay"
(U), 7.0 Mon. "The Silencers" (A).

WEST BROMWICH CINEMAS

QUEEN'S. WES. 0351. — "A
Shot in the Dark" (A), 5.5, 8.45,
"Pink Panther" (A) 6.45 (Sat. 2.0). Sun.
"Hercules Against Sons of the Sun" (x).

ABC. WES. 1210. — Cliff
Richard, "Summer Holiday" (U),
1.0, 4.45, 8.35. "Petticoat Pirates" (U),
2.50, 6.45. Sun. "Underworld U.S.A." (x).

Birmingham's
ELBOW ROOM
High St., Aston

Not a "Night Club" an
informal Late Bar (2 a.m.)
with Dancing, Buffet and in-
expensive GREEK speciality
Grills.
Cards and Roulette.
Location a few minutes
from the city centre on the
main Perry Barr, Walsall,
Manchester Road (A.34).
Music Programme and
Door Cover.
DISCS — MONDAY,
TUESDAY, THURSDAY.
No admission charge
GROUPS — WEDNESDAY
FRIDAY, SATURDAY.

The D'Fenders take delivery of their new van, from Burgess & Garfield, Stechford, 1966.

Fire and Safety Regulations

Will all bands please refrain from removing their equipment from the stage until 1am.

Carlton Johns Entertainments Ltd.
WISH THE
UGLY'S
Roger, Dave, James, Jimmy and Steve
EVERY SUCCESS on the release of their new record
END OF THE SEASON
A Ray Davies Composition
OUT SEPTEMBER 30th
Windermere House, 110, Wake Green Road, Moseley,
Birmingham, 13 :: Telephone 021 SOU 4097/8

FAN CLUBS
KEITH POWELL AND THE VALETS
FAN CLUB:
Secretary: Miss Carol Green
377 Stratford Road, Shirley
Solihull
'Phone: SHI 6924

BARBARA LINZ AND THE LEADERS
Manager: Mr. T. Sheppard
3 Cornwall Avenue, Quinton
Birmingham, 32
n Club: s.a.e. Miss P. Williams
Mansion Crescent, Smethwick

THE APPLEJACKS FAN CLUB
SUSAN
161 Redstone Farm Road
Hall Green, Birmingham, 28
MARINA
Castle Lane, Solihull, Warks.

FOR SALE
ORD THAMES MINIBUS
59, excellent condition: £180
Apply: Mr. B. Ennis
112 Broomhall Crescent
cocks Green, Birmingham, 27

Local Group, The Ugly's, 1966.

WE ARE
TOP PRIORITY
NOW, SAY
THE MARTELLS
STILL BOOKABLE THROUGH
CARLTON JOHNS
ENTERTAINMENTS LTD.
SOU 4097 — or
Management : C. A. A. BRECKNELL — MAY 2063

Clear The Track
Here Comes
THE
LOCOMOTIVE
Phone : MID 5210

THE GROUP WHO TRAVEL
ANYTIME/ANYWHERE
THE SHOOTING
STARS
Manager :
R. WHITTLESTONE.
141, TANHOUSE AVENUE,
BIRMINGHAM, 22a.
GRE 2912 : GRE 4538

Colmore Row, October 1966.

Chamberlain Square, 1966.

VAL DE TRAVERS

ASPHALTE
LIMITED

| Chester Street, Aston, Birmingham 6 | grams: Traversable phone: Aston Cross 1306 |

Digbeth STEEL

steel
stockholders
and
shearing
specialists

Digbeth
Steel
Stockholders
Limited

197-199
Bradford Street
Birmingham 12

Tel: Victoria
2227-8-9 · 6038-9

Telex 338594

Rostrevor Road/Hob Moor Road, Small Heath, 17th October 1966.

High Street, Erdington, October 1966.

Alum Rock Road, Saltley, 8th November 1966.

67

Goodrick Street, Nechells, 19th November 1966.

Assembly at St Anne's (C.E.) Junior & Infants' Voluntary Primary School is held in the Gaswork's Recreation Room next door, Devon Street, Nechells, 19th November 1966.

READY TO WEAR SUITS

Over 1,000 top grade suits in a wonderful selection of colours and designs. Superbly cut and tailored in all sizes and fittings up to 46in. chest, now being cleared at £££'s below usual retail prices.

MONOCRAFT TEXTILES

115 DALE END
BIRMINGHAM 4

HE'LL WIN HER
With a Gift of
PERFUME

from

M. GOODMAN
162 Aston Road
Birmingham 6

CAROUSEL RESTAURANT
SNOW HILL RINGWAY
BIRMINGHAM 4
Fully licensed restaurant and Steak Bar, with a pleasant informal atmosphere. Lamp service our speciality, light refreshments also available in Steak Bar. Diners catered for before and after the theatre.
Last orders taken at 10.30
Phone: CEN 1942

EVANS ELECTRONIC DEVELOPMENTS LTD.
Electronic and Scientific Equipment   Manufacturers of Industrial Electronic Equipment
Prototype and Production

EVONIC WORKS, SHADY LANE, BIRMINGHAM 22A
Tel.: GREat BARR 1764

Stratford Road, Sparkhill, 13th December 1966.

32 Bristol Street,   Studio MID 3792
Birmingham, 5.   Home JAMes Bridge 2413

LADBROOKE SOUND
RECORDING STUDIO
Full professional facilities at only 4 guineas per hour

Des O'Connor & Lynn Winters duet, "Puss In Boots" Alexandra Theatre, December 1966. This was producer, Derek Salberg's favourite pantomime.

BIRMINGHAM THEATRE
* **CHRISTMAS SEASON** *
Commencing MONDAY, 28th DECEMBER
Evenings 7.0 p.m.   Matinees 2.30 p.m.

TOM ARNOLD & BERNARD DELFONT
PRESENT

MORECAMBE & WISE
ERIC & ERNIE

in the magnificent pantomime

The Sleeping Beauty

with a terrific cast

★ ★ ★ ★ ★ ★ ★ ★ ★ ★ ★ ★ ★ ★
MAKE UP YOUR PARTY AND BOOK NOW

BOX OFFICE OPEN 10 a.m. - 9 p.m.   TELEPHONE MIDLAND 2576

In accordance with the requirements of the Licensing Justices.
(a) The public may leave at the end of the performance by all exits and entrances other than those used as queue waiting-rooms, and the doors of such exits and entrances shall at the time be open. (b) All gangways, passages, and staircases shall be kept entirely free from chairs or any other obstructions. (c) Persons shall not be permitted to stand or sit in any of the intersecting gangways. If standing be permitted at the rear of the seating, sufficient space shall be left for persons to pass easily to and fro. (d) The fireproof curtain shall at all times be maintained in working order and shall be lowered at the beginning of and during the time of every performance.

1967

Mr A L Cleverley, of British Eagle International Airlines Ltd., greets delegates from France prior to their college tour, January 1967.

Court Oak Road, Harborne, 1967.

The audience at the showing of "The Taming of the Shrew", includes, on the right, singer, Val Doonican and next to him, "Crossroads" actress, Noele Gordon, Odeon, New Street, 3rd March 1967. The event was in aid of the Cinema and Television Benevolent Fund.

H.M. GOVT. CONTRACTORS. A.I.D. Approved 1937

A.P. SPRINGS LIMITED

TRADE **APSCO** MARK

Manufacturers of
PRECISION SPRINGS
FOR ENGINEERING, MOTOR
ELECTRICAL & OTHER TRADES
PRESSWORK, NOVELTIES etc.

REDDINGS LANE,
SPARKHILL,
BIRMINGHAM 11
TEL: ACOCKS GREEN
2236-7-8 & 4195
GRAMS: ARPEN B'HAM

The last early morning rush hour at the original Snow Hill Station, 3rd March 1967.

ATKIN
& SONS (B'HAM) LIMITED
110 BRADFORD ST., 12

ESTABLISHED 1760
SAWS FOR WOOD AND METAL
SEGMENTAL AND HIGH-SPEED STEEL
SAWS SUPPLIED AND REPAIRED
MACHINE PLANING CUTTERS
BORING BITS & SAW MILL TOOLS
SPEEDY SAW REPAIR SERVICE

CIRCULAR
SAWS
& BAND SAWS
Phone
Victoria
3026
& 1840

Wheeler Street, Lozells, 11th April 1967. Spot the window cleaner?

Clifton Road/Upper Thomas Street, Aston, 30th June 1967.

Thomas Street, Aston, 6th July 1967.

A JOHN REEVE NIGHT SPOT

THE CASTAWAYS

THEATRE RESTAURANT AND NIGHT CLUB

ON STAGE THIS WEEK

EDMUND HOCKRIDGE

MEL PETERS ● FRENCH & JOY

PLUS

Peter Wheeler and his Music and the Waikiki Islanders
and to serve you 62 Castaway Girls

Dinner Show 8 p.m.-11.15 (Floor Show 9.30. Sun. 9 p.m.)
Supper Show 11.15-2 a.m. (Floor Show 12.30. Sun. 11 p.m.)

NEXT WEEK— LYNN ROGERS

Party Bookings Welcome. 'Phone 021 - 622 - 2421
BRADFORD HOUSE, BRADFORD STREET, BIRMINGHAM 5

CINEPHONE

FROM SUNDAY NEXT

A BAWDY, BUSTY BONANZA

WHEN THEY DRINK THE

VIRILE WATERS FROM THE

"FOUNTAIN OF LOVE"

'EVEN THE GRASS WENT GREEN WITH ENVY!'

SEX IN THE GRASS

EASTMAN COLOUR

4 performances daily at

12.45, 3.55, 6.20 & 9.10

But only 3 times on Sunday at **3.0, 5.35 & 8.10**

Upper Gough Street/Marshall Street, July 1967.

Titecast Limited

RECLAMATION OF POROUS CASTINGS IN ALL METALS

2 RAILWAY ARCH, FAZELEY STREET, BIRMINGHAM.

Telephone : Midland 4609

Head Office : 123A GORTON RD. REDDISH, STOCKPORT, CHESHIRE.

Telephone : Heaton Moor 8700

BRANCHES AT: GATESHEAD, SLOUGH & STOCKPORT

I'LL MISS . . .

WHAT I shall miss is the Sunday Citizen's inspiring articles on the working-class movement and the decent standards of living everyone is entitled to; especially your article last Sunday on "Life Under £15 a Week," which thousands have to manage on. I agree with Frank Cousins when he says everybody should have a minimum wage of £15 a week after all stoppages are taken out.

You always spoke out forthright, even against this Government when needed. The Labour Government have done some good things, passed some good Acts, but they went wrong in not giving our paper advertisements and the SET tax on the Co-ops and other concerns as well. I don't think they acted at all well towards the Citizen or the Co-ops.

I think this Government has made a lot of bad friends amongst Co-op members and union members amongst our own class; though I like the Prime Minister. Harold Wilson keeps on fighting.—**George T. Betts**, Birmingham.

Soho Road, Handsworth, July 1967.

Members of the Midlands' Branch of the Incorporated Association of Architects' and Surveyors' Committee, 1967.

KINGS HEATH HORSE SHOW

TYTHE BARN LANE, EARLSWOOD

SUNDAY, JULY 16th 1967

Ringside Parking £1
Admission 4/- Children and O.A.P. 2/-
Car Parking 2/-

Become a Member of the Midlands' oldest
Established Horse Show Society

Annual Membership Fee £1 1s. 0d.

Applications for membership to the Secretary
Mrs. Betty Hollies
34, Dudley Road
Brades Village
Oldbury

Telephone: Broadwell 3109

PHILLIPS *Signs*

Studio: 3-45 POPLAR ROAD
KING'S HEATH, BIRMINGHAM 14

Ansafone/Telephone 021-444 2970

YARDLEYS

NEW ORCHESTRAL INSTRUMENT DEPT NOW OPEN

TRUMPETS
TROMBONES
SAXOPHONES
CLARINETS
OBOES
FLUTES

Midland Distributors
for
Besson, Boosey,
Selmer, Buisston,
Le Blanc, Conn,
Buescher and all
other Leading Makes

and ALL BRASS BAND INSTRUMENTS and ACCESSORIES

DRUM DEPARTMENT
LARGEST STOCKS IN BRITAIN of
PREMIER — LUDWIG — ROGERS
OTHER OUTFITS *from* £25
GENEROUS PART EXCHANGE ALLOWANCES

GUITARS & AMPLIFIERS

VOX - MARSHALL - SELMER
BURNS & ALL OTHER MAKES
5 Watt — 200 Watt

MICROPHONES
£5 to £35
and ALL OTHER EQUIPMENT

⊙ HIRE PURCHASE FACILITIES AVAILABLE ⊙
87 – 89 SNOW HILL. BIRMINGHAM 4

NEXT TO Y.M.C.A. ———— CEN 7441

Aston Brook Street, Aston, 25th July 1967.

Hope Street, Highgate, 1967.

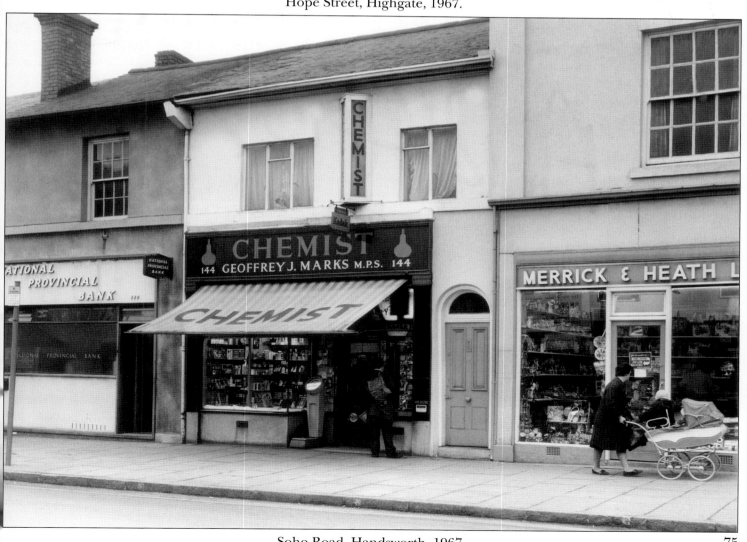

Soho Road, Handsworth, 1967.

Bracebridge Street, Aston, 25th July 1967.

Orchard Road, Balsall Heath, 22nd August 1967.

HAROLD E. PEACE & CO. LTD.

TRANSFER PRINTERS

T.A. "HEPACO"
T.N. CENTRAL 3781 & 3782
22 & 36 LUDGATE HILL,
BIRMINGHAM 3

"THE EXCELSIOR ARTISTS"
AGENCY

618 Stratford Road, Sparkhill
Birmingham, 11
'Phone: SPR 6280
ACO 2049 is Private 'phone and Home Address only
Managing Director: RICHARD HOMANS—Office Hrs.

Dances, Parties, Weddings and
Concerts
JON E. LAW and
The Trespassers Rhythm Group
Manager: Mr. D. W. Garner
65 Romsley Road, Bartley Green
Birmingham, 32   Tel.: PRI 6431

WOT—NO GROUP?
Then book
"THE CHADS"
T. Warrender
SPR 3777 - SPR 2016

For the Best in Beat, book
THE ROCKIN' MARTELLS
featuring
LEE WILDER
'Phone: MAYpole 2063
Manager: Mr. C. A. A. Brecknell

JENNY ALLEN with the
CADENZAS
The Midlands' top girl singer and
her fabulous backing group
Sole management: Dick Jaffa
EDG 1536 - HAR 2149

Feeling let down . . .
You should have used the
THE CIMARRONS
(Dial Records)
Rubery 2923 and 3276

DECCA RECORDING ARTISTES
THE REDCAPS
All enquiries:
Mrs. Regan, c/o Plaza Ballroom
Rookery Road, Handsworth
Birmingham, 21

RENEGADES
of Birmingham
BIRCHFIELD 6667

"DIAL" RECORDING ARTISTES

"BRUM BEAT" L.P.

Publicity: Michael McGrath
(Alma Cogan, Eden Kane,
Mark Wynter, etc.)

Conybere Street, Highgate, 25th September 1967.

Rear of Crawford Street, Saltley, 25th October 1967.

Spencer Street/Northampton Street, Hockley, 1967.

77

GEC, Witton, 1967.

Part of the GEC Witton works, Electric Avenue, 25th October 1967.

FOR THE GIRL WHO WEARS THE TROUSERS

A snazzy outfit that really will command attention whether it is used for day or evening wear. It's made of Acrilan, another point in its favour, and is available in Navy Blue. Sizes 34in.-38in.
PRICE £7-10-0

MISS DOMINO   SECOND FLOOR

Rackhams
CORPORATION STREET   BIRMINGHAM

CENtral 3333

T. J. LOCK
184 Alum Rock Rd., Birmingham 8
PHONE: EAS 1350

NEWSAGENTS TOBACCONISTS STATIONERS

BOOKS, MAGAZINES ETC

A Wide Range of Greeting Cards for Every Occasion.

"A Card Costs So Little But Means So Much."

BRENDA
Ladies', Children's & Baby Wear
784 COVENTRY ROAD
"Ladybird" Agency
Wool — Hosiery

TELEPHONE VIC 3297

Alcester Road South, Kings Heath, 16th November 1967.

The Candy Box
Newsagents & Confectioners
782 COVENTRY ROAD

Christmas Cards, Books, Children's Annuals.

It's Surprising What You Can Get at

SHAKESPEARE'S
"The Shops by The Lights"

GREETINGS CARDS FOR EVERY POSSIBLE OCCASION
NEWSPAPERS, PERIODICALS, BOOKS, MAGAZINES, STATIONERY, TOYS,
GAMES, FANCY GOODS, CONFECTIONERY, ETC.

2233 COVENTRY ROAD and 3 SHEAF LANE, SHELDON
Telephone SHE 2092

Gerrard Street, with Wheeler Street coming up, Lozells, 11th December 1967.

NEON GLASSCRAFTS for NEON SIGNS

(PROPRIETORS : F. WATSON, G. BAKER)

QUICK REPAIRS — INSTALLATIONS — RENOVATIONS — MAINTENANCE

Office and Works : 63 WATER STREET, BIRMINGHAM 3   TELEPHONE : CEN. 1793

Greenway Street, Small Heath, 1967.

RE-UPHOLSTERY

Ladies! Would you like your present suite to be the envy of your guests at Christmas?
There is still time for you to choose from a range of 500 patterns and a wide selection of materials.
Loose covers a speciality Estimates at your convenience and without obligation. Collection and delivery free
QUALITY UPHOLSTERY
Ring:
MID 8686 any time

TYPEWRITERS

Beat The Import Levy
Just 25 Portable Typewriters left, at pre-levy prices. Save 15 per cent, cash or terms, from 21/- deposit and 5/- per week. Office models from 70/- cash, fully guaranteed.
COUNTY OFFICE
EQUIPMENT LIMITED
204 CORPORATION STREET
CEN 4281
(Opposite Law Courts)
Also at
825 STRATFORD ROAD
SPARKHILL. SPR 5246
(Opposite Springfield Ballroom)
Both shops open till 8 p.m. Friday

MARY'S
DOG PARLOUR
All breeds stripped and trimmed. For appointment Phone ACO 1751

CAVALRY TWILL
TROUSERS
All - wool heavyweight s l a c k s immaculately tailored in Fawn, Lovat and Bronze shades. All sizes up to 42 in. waist. Normal retail price 5 gns. now being cleared at 55/-.
MONOCRAFT
TEXTILES
115 DALE END
BIRMINGHAM 4

PRETTY BABY!
The Kiddies Shop way.
SHOP LOCALLY
at The Kiddies' Shop
No need to go into Town
The Kiddies' Shop, 362 Birmingham Road, Wylde Green, have EVERYTHING for Children at FAIR PRICES

GIVE HIM
a good start every morning with a new battery from:
THE BATTERY SHOP
182 BROMSGROVE ST.
MID 1187
(Opp. New Ice Rink)

1968

GENUINE SALE DIRECT TO THE PUBLIC, OF

SURPLUS GOVERNMENT, CORPORATION AND G.P.O. STOCK AT FRACTIONAL COST

BUS DRIVERS' WATERPROOF MACKINTOSHES. **25/-**
Navy blue. At each
MEN'S WORKING TROUSERS. **7/6**
At per pair
MEN'S KHAKI WAIST LENGTH DUSTCOATS. **3/6**
At each
PAINT. Super quality Hard Gloss. Colour red, in **59/6**
5-gallon drums. Per 5-gallon drum
Also Stone colour in Hard Gloss in 5-gall. drums.
Per 5-gall drum 59/6
NYLON TUBING. ⅜in o.d. 250ft. coils. Brand **12/6**
new. Per coil
DUNLOP RUBBER ANKLE BOOTS. Lace-up, new. **10/-**
Size 6 only Per Pair
TELEPHONES. Ex-G.P.O. **10/-**
Each
TELEPHONE SETS. Type F, Mark 2. **£5-10-0**
Including batteries. Per pair
MATCHETS. In Scabbard (Grade 1). **15/-**
Each
DOUBLE TIER BUNKS. Steel. **69/6**
Each

ALL THE ABOVE ITEMS ARE GUARANTEED GENUINE GOVERNMENT OR MINISTRY STOCK

Available from:—
WOOTTON'S
(Government Surplus Contractors)
1072, COVENTRY ROAD, HAY MILLS, BIRMINGHAM 25
(Opposite Kings Road) TELEPHONE: 772 3119

CHERRY WALLPAPERS
SALE NOW ON!

LAST FEW SPECIAL OFFERS!

PERMOGLAZE Brilliant White EMULSION PAINT QUART **8/11**
GAY WASHABLES Large Selection. FROM PER ROLL **4/11**

Modern BLOCK DESIGN WALLPAPER Per Roll **3/11**
EMBOSSED ABSTRACT PATTERN Per Roll **7/6**
GOLD STRIPE Effect WALLPAPER Per Roll **6/11**
HEAVY FLORAL Design WALLPAPER Per Roll **9/11**
FLORAL STRIPE PATTERN Per Roll **3/11**

40% OFF
MANUFACTURER'S RECOMMENDED RETAIL PRICES
ICI **VYMURA**
VINYL WALLCOVERING
1969/70 PATTERNS.
ALL PERFECT STOCK. From **16/11** PER ROLL

Modern MEDALLION EFFECT Per Roll **4/11**
HEAVY EMBOSSED Abstract Pattern. Per Roll **6/11**
MICA CEILING PAPER Per Roll **2/11**
PEBBLE CEILING PAPER Per Roll **6/11**
TRADITIONAL SQUARE Suitable wall or ceiling **7/11**

WE HAVE THE LARGEST SELECTION OF 1969 PATTERNS IN THE MIDLANDS

Cherry Wallpapers
CHERRY STREET CITY CENTRE Tel: MID. 7234
249 HIGH STREET ERDINGTON Tel: 373 6725
233 ALUM ROCK RD. ALUM ROCK Tel: EAS. 1724
135 HIGH STREET, KINGS HEATH Tel: 444 5283

Sherbourne Road, Balsall Heath, 30th January 1968.

Balsall Heath Road, 30th January 1968.

The British Motor Corporation Ltd., Longbridge, c 1968. To this day locals refer to it as "The Austin".

THE B·M·C DRIVERS' CLUB

Safe Driving Award

MADE BY THE CLUB TO

.................Mr. R.T. Dillon............ MEMBER No. 163.953

FOR HAVING BEEN FREE FROM ACCIDENTS FOR WHICH HE WAS
IN ANY WAY BLAMEWORTHY WHILST DRIVING A MECHANICALLY PROPELLED
VEHICLE DURING THE PAST THREE YEARS AND THUS CONTRIBUTING
TO ROAD SAFETY IN ACCORDANCE WITH THE AIMS OF THE CLUB

DATED 12 - 2 - 68.   NATIONAL ORGANIZER

RESULTS COUNT
80% PASS ON FIRST TEST

IT COSTS LESS TO LEARN QUICKLY
WITH

WEST MIDLAND DRIVING SCHOOL
(FREE DOOR - TO - DOOR SERVICE)
9 - 11 WATFORD ROAD, KINGS NORTON.
Telephone : KIN 2464

FOR MOTORISTS IS THE BEST SEASON OF THE YEAR

SPRING

JOHN SPRING
(INSURANCES) LTD.
8 STONEY LANE, SPARKHILL
VIC 1880 and 4661/2   BIRMINGHAM 11

ACKNOWLEDGED TO BE BEST FOR ALL FORMS OF INSURANCE.
OUR COMPREHENSIVE COVER EVERY TYPE OF MOTORING
ACCIDENTS, AND ALL CLAIMS RECEIVE PROMPT ATTENTION

SPECIAL REBATE! CAREFUL DRIVERS ARE ALLOWED A 50 PER CENT. NO CLAIM BONUS

185 HEATHFIELD ROAD   233 WALSALL ROAD
HANDSWORTH   NOR 3472   PERRY BARR 22b   BIR 4193

WE SPECIALISE IN MOTOR INSURANCE, HIRE PURCHASE, CONTRACT BONDS AND PENSION SCHEMES.

SAFETY FIRST - - MIND THAT CHILD !

Moseley Road, with Belgrave Road at the top, 1968.

A PREMIUM SHOE SERVICE
as New!

Long soled and heeled in leather or any
of the proprietary makes of synthetics
and rubber.

Re-welting, re-lining, re-colouring, first-
class material, real craft workmanship

ANY PAYNES
REPAIR SHOP WILL ACCEPT YOUR
ORDER FOR FORWARDING TO
THE PREMIUM REPAIR CENTRE

HARRY H. PAYNE LTD., LONGMORE HOUSE, CROMER ROAD, B'HAM 12
Telephone : SOUth 3751

BILL HOWARD (KITTS GREEN) LTD.
Agent for all leading makes Cycles, Motor-Cycles, Side-cars and Scooters.

70 East Meadway, Kitts Green, Birmingham, 33   Tel.: STE 6176

BILL HOWARD (Sheldon) LTD.
Agent for all Motor-Cycles, Sidecars, Scooters.
2335 COVENTRY ROAD SHELDON, BIRMINGHAM, 26
SHE 3506

HOWARD & ROUND LTD.
MAJESTIC BUILDINGS, FIVE WAYS
CRADLEY HEATH.   Tel. 69366

MANY NEW AND USED MACHINES IN STOCK ALL LEADING MAKES IN STOCK

A sterling service for every Motorist

ENTIRE MIDLAND AREA COVERED

B. J. W.
MOTOR ENGINEERS

Complete overhauls, Electrical Repairs,
Wiring, Lighting, etc.

Servicing, Rebores, Tuning.

Reduced rates for Fleet Operators.

Write or call:
188 Witton Road, Aston, Birmingham, 6.

Salford Bridge, 1968.

Gerrard Street, Lozells, 11th March 1968.

GO TENPIN BOWLING

AT THE

ABC CINE-bowl

STIRCHLEY
KINGS NORTON 4444
OPEN WEEKDAYS from 10 a.m.
SATS and SUNS from 9 a.m.
CAR PARK · GRILLETTE · LICENSED CLUB
You can book your lane in advance

Price of Games:
6.30 p.m. to 11.30 p.m.
and all day Sunday 3/6d
per game.
Other times: Adults
2/6d per game; Children
1/6d per game.

St Philip's Churchyard, 1st June 1968.

Opening of Howard Electric, by ventriloquist, Terry Hall, Old Walsall Road, Great Barr, August 1968.

P.J. ALLPORT & CO.

LAND, HOUSE & ESTATE AGENTS & VALUERS.

131 SOHO HILL 19
TEL. NORTHERN 4071.

Michael Vincent and the Directors of

TREASURE TROVE (BIRMINGHAM) LTD.

invite you to the official opening of their

𝔄ntique and 𝔙ictorian 𝔐arket

by

Miss Noele Gordon

Star of A.T.V's "Crossroads"

at

1852/4 PERSHORE ROAD, COTTERIDGE on

TUESDAY, 27th AUGUST 1968 at 10-30 a.m.

JOSEPH GILMAN & SON LTD.

Manufacturers of
'NONPAREIL' & 'GLASSARD' CASE HARDENING COMPOUNDS & CARBURISING SOLUTIONS

'PHONE: CENTRAL 6652 (4 lines)
'GRAMS: 'GLUE', B'HAM 19.

SHADWELL HOUSE
LOWER LOVEDAY STREET
BIRMINGHAM 19.

Some of the contents of the Treasure Trove, Pershore Road, Cotteridge, 1968.

BRUNTONS (MUSSELBURGH) LTD.
MUSSELBURGH SCOTLAND

BIRMINGHAM OFFICE
HAMMOND HOUSE,
2259-61 COVENTRY RD.
SHELDON 26
She 5271/2; Telex 33733

WIRE ROPE
also manufacturers of
COLD ROLLED STEEL STRIP.
FLATTENED WIRE,
SPRING WIRE (ALL GRADES)
STAINLESS STEEL, BRIGHT DRAWN
BARS, SPECIAL DRAWN SECTIONS,
SILVER STEEL, HIGH SPEED STEEL,
MUSIC WIRE, ARMATURE WIRE

Young Masters Limited

ASTon 2644 **YM**

Shopfitters
165 Park Lane
Aston
Birmingham 6

CHARLES T. DOBSON LTD.
297 CORPORATION ST. BIRMINGHAM·4
TEL. AST. 1419 ESTABLISHED 1901

SCRAP IRON STEEL & METAL MERCHANTS

Couzens and Akers Ltd. (heating engineers),
Aston Road, Aston, 1968.

MECCA LTD

ROLLER RINK DE LUXE

000346

THE OLYMPIC
SUMMERHILL ROAD BIRMINGHAM   TELEPHONE CEN. 0388-9

The Rink Manager, MR. CLIVE PRESTON would like you to be his guest on
WEDNESDAY OCTOBER 16 'Over 18 Night'

It's great to Skate
at the finest Roller Rink in the world. It's dust and noise free, on the finest Maple Floor. Finest
Boots and Skates to hire. Hasty Tasty Buffet. Rolarena Bar. Equal to a Mecca Dance Hall.
No. 8 Bus to Spring Hill or B82 or B83 Bus from town.   Doors Open and Skating from 7.30 p.m.
ONLY THE "SILENT" SKATES AVAILABLE IN THE RINK CAN BE USED
GUEST TICKET—ADMIT ONE   No admission under 18 years of age.   To be given up at Box Office

- -

The Management reserve the right to refuse admission

Kindly retain this portion
of your ticket for use in
the cloakroom.   Fee 6d.

000346

★ EXPERT TAILORING REPAIRS
READY IN ONLY 4 DAYS

★ DE-LUXE SHIRT LAUNDRY
36 HOUR SERVICE

Discriminating people choose

JANET LEONARD
34 HIGH ST., SALTLEY (Next to Gate Inn)
Telephone: EAS 4104

49/11d.

N. MUNDY LTD.
BULL RING BALCONY
Finest selection in Town
of Shoes, Boots and
Slippers for that extra
Christmas Gift.

Phone: MID 1512.

EVERYTHING FOR THE HOME
DECORATOR
Stockists of the Leading Brands of Paints
and Wallpapers

LEE BROS.
SELLY OAK
53 Raddlebarn Road, Selly Oak
Birmingham 29.   SEL 1710

ADVICE GLADLY GIVEN ON ALL YOUR
DECORATING PROBLEMS

A champagne party to celebrate the arrival of the first No.43 bus in Bull Street, October 1968. After more than 20
years part of the road, from Corporation Street to Colmore Row, was opened to two-way traffic.

Lee Bank Road, 2nd November 1968.

The Lady Mayoress, Mrs Charles Simpson, pays a Christmas visit to Pegasus Infants' School,
Castle Vale, 6th December 1968.

Great Western Arcade, looking towards Snow Hill Station, 1969.

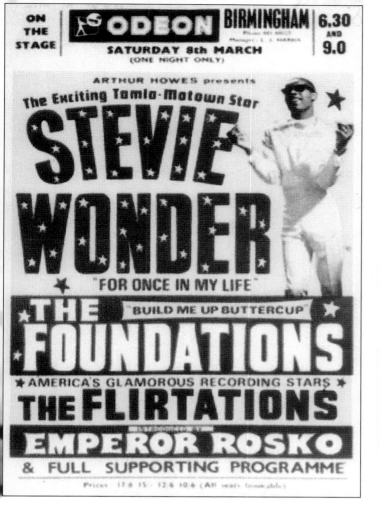

ON THE STAGE

ODEON BIRMINGHAM

SATURDAY 8th MARCH
(ONE NIGHT ONLY)

6.30 AND 9.0

ARTHUR HOWES presents

The Exciting Tamla-Motown Star

STEVIE WONDER

"FOR ONCE IN MY LIFE"

THE FOUNDATIONS
"BUILD ME UP BUTTERCUP"

★ AMERICA'S GLAMOROUS RECORDING STARS ★

THE FLIRTATIONS

EMPEROR ROSKO

& FULL SUPPORTING PROGRAMME

Prices 17/6 15/- 12/6 10/6 (All seats bookable)

PUNCH MACHINE OPERATORS

Girls, 15 years of age, required for large office, Central Premises. The successful applicants will be given all round training in this type of work. Wage, plus bonus. Good conditions of employment.

Applications in writing in the first instance to the

PERSONNEL OFFICER

BIRMINGHAM CO-OPERATIVE SOCIETY LTD.

10 Castle Street, off High Street, Birmingham 4

Capt Jordan, of the Church Army, discusses tennis with his youth club members, Heath Street, Winson Green, July 1969.

HAVEN'T got anything to wear. Make this a saying of your past. C. W. Sutton, 441 Stratford Road, Birmingham 11, provide selections of ladies', dresses, jumpers and lingerie at reasonable prices.

Flowers for every occasion home and abroad
DOROTHY FRAZIER LTD.,
133 ALCESTER ROAD,
MOSELEY
Tel. SOU 4894
Interflora Florist

TWO hours after landing on the moon last night Neil Armstrong and Edwin Aldrin decided that they would step on to the lunar surface at 2 o'clock this morning.

Mission Control in Houston, Texas, signalled: "O.K.—we are ready to support you on that."

The moon walk was brought forward by 5 hours 12 minutes mainly because Armstrong and Aldrin were in tremendous form.

But there was also some concern about possible trouble from pressure in the fuel pipes of the descent engine.

To commemorate the historic Moon landing the Man in the Moon is re-christened the Man on the Moon, Redditch Road, West Heath, July 1969.

GOULD & BROWNE
chartered surveyors

45 NEWHALL STREET
BIRMINGHAM 3, CEN 1946/7

Branch Office : 3a Station Approach
Dorridge, Solihull
Knowle 4878

91

Music Class, Yardley Wood Junior School, School Road, 1969.

Kings Norton Green, 1969.

SHOPFITTINGS

T. SAVEKER Ltd.

make all types of
Shop fitters' Metalwork

PHILLIPS ST., BIRMINGHAM 6

Tel.: Aston Cross 5891 (5 lines)
Comprehensive catalogues on request

Old Square, 26th August 1969.

REGISTERED OFFICE :
CLAPGATE LANE
BIRMINGHAM 32

PHONE :
WOODGATE
021-422 3414-5-6

CLASSIC ENGINEERING
LTD.

MANUFACTURERS OF
MOTOR and AIRCRAFT
SHEET METAL PARTS
PANEL BEATING and
PANEL WHEELING A
SPECIALITY

Dancing to The Modernaires, The Mackadown, Mackadown Lane, Sheldon, 1969. Due to their popularity the group appeared at the same venue on dozens of occasions.

After the show . .
Dine at the

Tung Fong

Chinese Restaurant

Proprietor : LENA WOO

64-66, Hurst Street

(3 minutes from this theatre)

—

SPECIALISTS IN ENGLISH AND CHINESE DISHES

Open 12 noon until 11-30 p.m.

—

Telephone reservations accepted
Phone : MID 0666

MIKE CARROLL

presents

"THE GREATEST"

THIS AND EVERY WEDNESDAY NIGHT

TWO SENSATIONAL GROUPS EVERY WEEK

For the best on the Midland Beat Scene, it's the

MACKADOWN

MACKADOWN LANE, KITTS GREEN, BIRMINGHAM, 33

'Bus from City No. 14

But like the man said: " Please don't be late "

Birmingham-born actor, Raymond Huntley, 1969. A regular in films and TV dramas, throughout the sixties, he started his career at the Repertory Theatre.

ENTERTAINERS.

MADGE E. KWAND I.B.M., S.M.S.

4 Station rd 14.   T N Highbury 2494

DIXON'S

Established 1853   Late   Great Barr Street

1090 COVENTRY ROAD
HAY MILLS

—

Branches .

317 WYNDHURST ROAD
STECHFORD

180 GREEN LANE
SMALL HEATH

ALL THE LEADING CHECKS ACCEPTED

for

● LADIES' & CHILDRENS' OUTFITTING
● JEWELLERY
● MATTING AND RUGS
● BOOTS, SHOES, ETC.

Dancers from the "Arcadians", Birmingham Theatre, 14th September 1969. In 1965 Moss Empires had renamed it, but this was never accepted by the public and in 1972 it reverted to the name we had all continued to use – the Hippodrome.

Aldridge Road, Perry Barr, c1969.

UNIVERSAL

The latest "SewMaid" NEW From Factory to You

STYLISH 2-COLOUR
SMARTLY STREAMLINED

VARIED STITCHES
STYLISH COVER
ELECTRIC BOBBIN WINDER
TENSION SETTER
MOTOR BY US!
SMART BASE
LOCKSTITCH

£11.19.6 CASH

EASY TERMS
PART EXCHANGES

FREE DELIVERY
IN VAN SERVICE AREA

Write, 'phone or call — NOW !

UNIVERSAL SEWING MACHINES LTD.
(P.O. BOX 141) 27-33 HURST ST., B'HAM 5
'Phone: MID 7901

Lionel Acton-Hubbard, of the British Temperance Movement, gives an anti-smoking lecture, Trafalgar House, Paradise Street, 16th September 1969.

Alcester Road, Moseley, 1969.

Demolition of the Great Western Hotel, Colmore Row, 23rd October 1969.

Back Cover: Bull Street, with Temple Row on the left, 17th October 1962.

ACKNOWLEDGEMENTS

(for providing photographs, encouragement and numerous other favours)

Keith Ackrill; Peter Ashlington; Norman Bailey; The Birmingham City Council Dept. of Planning and Architecture; The Birmingham Post and Mail Ltd; Arthur Brown; John and Maisie Brown; The late Arthur Camwell; Wilf Clare; Roy Dillon; Paula Earle; Tony Eaton; Ray Green; Joyce Hargreaves; Derek Horner; Vernon Jones; Royston Kemp; Midland Beat; Dennis Moore; Gertrude and Alan Peters; Brian Pinkerton; Keith and Stella Price; Arthur Radburn; Howard Reeves; Dave Robinson; Geoffrey Round; Jim Simpson; Len Thompson; Michael Vincent; Joan Wanty; Rosemary Wilkes; Anne Williams; Keith Williams; Ken Windsor.

Please forgive any possible omissions. Every effort has been made to include all organisations and individuals involved in the book.

Father Thomas Rocks appeal for trading stamps receives a great response, St Martin's de Porres, Moseley, 3rd July 1968. The money raised was to buy a house for the homeless.